WOMEN
OF FAITH & SPIRIT
Profiles of Fifteen Biblical Witnesses

Margaret Wold

AUGSBURG Publishing House • Minneapolis

WOMEN OF FAITH AND SPIRIT
Profiles of 15 Biblical Witnesses

Library of Congress Cataloging-in-Publication Data

Wold, Marge.
  WOMEN OF FAITH AND SPIRIT.

  Bibliography: p.
  1. Women in the Bible—Biography.   2. Bible—
Biography.   I. Title.
BS575.W59   1987   220.9'2   [B]   86-28770
ISBN 0-8066-2251-2

Manufactured in the U.S.A.   APH 10-7236

   3   4   5   6   7   8   9   0   1   2   3   4   5   6   7   8   9

CONTENTS

INTRODUCTION

Women are rediscovering each other. With the disappearance of the smaller, more supportive communities of the past, women have become more isolated in urban and suburban settings. We are at a time in history when women are searching to find out all they can about themselves.

In the journey toward mutual discovery, the stories of the personal strength and stalwart faith of our foremothers have become a source of encouragement in our ongoing pilgrimage. For Christian women, the stories of our faith-sisters recorded in the Bible provide rich resources for understanding ourselves, our church, and our God.

These sisters in the faith stand out boldly among that "great cloud of witnesses" cheering us on, encouraging us to "run with perseverance the race that is set before us . . . " (Heb. 12:1). In this study we step into their lives with excitement and respect.

The Bible and the Stories of Women

The Bible is inspired. It is the work of many authors, written over a 1600-year span of time. The Old Testament was written in Hebrew and the New Testament in Greek. Although it was written by human beings, we accept the Bible as God's Word and the writers as inspired by God's Spirit. Since most of us do not read the original languages of the Bible, we must accept the translation as inspired, understanding that sometimes words in other languages have slightly different meanings.

Because the Bible writers lived during different historical periods, we will have to examine the cultural and historical settings in which they wrote. Their perceptions of the events they relate were affected by the times in which they lived. Certainly what they wrote about women was influenced by the fact that they were men in a patriarchal society.

A patriarchal society is one in which the government is by men. The root meaning of the word *patriarchy* is "rule by the fathers." The father (or the male heir of his choice) rules. In such a society, property is handed down from father to son to grandson, but women have few rights. Women are considered the property of men and are passed on from father to husband or to their brothers or husband's brothers as circumstances dictate. Men, simply because they are men, have unearned privileges in a patriarchal society.

In biblical times the world was not an easy one for women. Our foremothers were valued primarily for their sexual attractiveness, their ability to please their husbands, and their ability to produce children, especially sons. They could be divorced for little reason (Deut. 24:1-4) but could not sue for divorce themselves even if they were cruelly mistreated by their spouses.

Our Amazing Foremothers!

What remarkable people they are, these Bible women! In spite of the political, economic, educational, and religious restrictions of their day, they left us tremendous examples of faith, achievement, and endurance! They not only survived and triumphed personally, but they left their legacy to the people of God and to the history of salvation.

In these stories of biblical women of faith are hidden our own tears and laughter, our anger and joy, our exaltation and despair, but always we will perceive ourselves in new ways as one in faith with the women of the Bible, children of God made in the image of the Creator, one with women of faith in every time and place.

Jesus and Women

With the birth of Jesus, the religious history of women changed dramatically. His behavior toward women was a radical departure from many of the cultural norms of the previous eras and from many of the customs of his own culture. He called women to the same life of devotion to God as men, affirming their value as his followers. He never denied them any of his gifts—healing, teaching, resurrection power.

The Christian era really began with the first appearance of Jesus after the resurrection, the appearance to Mary Magdalene and the other women at the tomb. Although their witness as women was not accepted in the patriarchal community of that time, Bible history has recorded their testimony.

The Format

Each study of the women of the Bible will include the following sections:

The Setting

A description of the cultural setting and historical period in which the woman under discussion lived and her role in that setting.

The Story

A telling of the story of the woman who is the focus of our attention in the chapter.

The Summary

A commentary on the Bible narrative and the implications of the story for the lives of Christian women in our time.

To supplement the biblical portrayals of the women we will be meeting, this study includes Bible passages, scholarly sources, and the writer's personal reflections. Let your imagination help bring life to your understanding of these biblical women. You are encouraged to learn to know them very well. They are your sisters in the faith.

Begin your personal study by reading the assigned Scripture texts. The Revised Standard Version of the Bible is the recommended text.

Genesis 1:27-31; 2:18-24; 3:1—4:2

EVE

The Setting: Beginnings

We must depend heavily on the Bible itself for any description of the setting for the story of Eve. No one but God was there before the creation of Adam and Eve. Our biblical account depends on an oral tradition common among people who were closer in time to those events than we are. Such people listened to their fathers and mothers tell the stories as they heard them from *their* fathers and mothers and as they in turn had heard them from *their* parents. Poets and professional storytellers may also have entertained others with their more highly polished versions of the age-old stories.

Naturally much curiosity surrounds the origin of things and peoples. Firsts of anything are always intriguing. "Was there really one man and woman in the beginning?" we ask. "What did they look like? What language did they speak?" Although there are many hypotheses about the origin of the universe and the development of the human race, we are going to take the biblical accounts as they are recorded and do our best to understand the woman Eve in that recorded setting. We will be reflecting theologically and imaginatively on the events we read about.

At the same time we do not want to ignore the literary realities of the Bible record and one of the first realities to become apparent to us is that the first three chapters of Genesis contain two separate versions of creation. The first version takes us through Chapter 1 and the first three and one-half verses of Chapter 2.

Many students of the Bible believe that this account was added as an introductory chapter to Genesis after the Babylonian captivity of the Jews when it was written down from the oral tradition. This account is primarily doctrine, carefully thought through for its theological implications. The form is poetic and profoundly simple. It represents centuries of reflection on the creation story.

Chapter 2:4b through Chapter 3 has an entirely different form and feeling. Some readers may find this account much easier to read since the storyteller uses more descriptive words, dialog, and action. This work is probably the much older account.

While Chapter 1 describes the events of seven days of creation with an orderly progression from "lower" to "higher" forms of life, Chapter 2 has the creation of man, earth, heavens, vegetation, beasts, birds, and woman occur all in one day. In Chapter 1, humankind was created last; in Chapter 2, man and woman were created immediately after the earth itself. Obviously, nothing can be proved then from any specific order in creation.

In Chapter 1 there is a simultaneous appearance of man and woman. In Chapter 1 the Hebrew word for ground is *'adamah,* (pronounced to rhyme with "ma-ma-ma," with the accent on the last "ma") and the person(s) made in the image of God is *'adam* (pronounced "ah-dahm" with the accent on the second syllable).

Only in Chapter 2, verse 23, do man *(ish)* and woman *(ishshah)* become two distinct persons. Both man and woman find their ultimate identity in the being of God in whom all the characteristics of humanity must be found.

Where was the garden of Eden in which, according to Genesis 2, our first parents lived? It seems clear that the writer had some definite place in mind. The mystery of its location intrigues the imagination. Genesis 2:8-15 gives enough clues to suggest a particular place. The Tigris and the Euphrates rivers can be located, but the other rivers are lost in antiquity. The best guesses about the garden's whereabouts seem to place it near the source of the Tigris and Euphrates somewhere in the Armenian highlands.

More important than its location is the symbolism of a garden. Our oneness with the earth from which we are made is most evident in a garden. Tending the soil, coming in contact with our "roots," has healing power, and gardens are good places to walk and talk of God. A garden with green, growing things, with birds singing and woodland creatures sporting with one another—is this not paradise? To nomadic people of the desert in constant search of water, the vision of an oasislike garden must have exerted a strong pull toward the God who met people there.

In the story, the fruit of one of the trees in the garden was forbidden for food. We read that when Adam and Eve ate of the fruit, a simple act of disobedience was committed. As a result the entire human race came under bondage to sin and death. The only "new knowledge" Adam and Eve got after eating the fruit was their awareness of nakedness and an accompanying sense of shame. This sense of shame and guilt penetrates to the innermost depths of human existence. The compulsion to cover their bodies and to hide from God tainted the glory of the image of God in those first human beings. The psalmist weeps over this reality in Psalm 51:5,

Behold, I was brought forth in iniquity,
and in sin did my mother conceive me.

As we reflect on the story, we need to think about our own sexuality and the wholeness we know God intends for us.

The Story: Creation of Eve

(Since the Bible does not tell us much about Eve as a person, much of the following story is based on personal reflection and conjecture. Challenge it, check it out, but do think about this first woman and draw your own conclusions as to what she might have thought and felt.)

Only Genesis 2 tells us about Eve. Certainly, in the mind of this storyteller, she came perfect from the Creator's mind and hands.

As the result of a high school English class assignment, a 16-year-old girl wrote the following poem to Eve:

O how can pen e'er tell the charm and grace
Of woodland nymph in sylvan everglade,

Of moonbeams cold which weave the trees to lace,
Of thou beside whom e'en the light would fade?
Beauty, for her thy name is much too small,
In whom encompassed are the charms of all.

Underneath the poem's sentimentality pulses a young woman's longing to discover the source of her being. That 16-year-old girl struggling with her dawning self-consciousness represents every woman in the dawn of self-understanding. How did Eve understand her own being?

Genesis 1:27 informs us that God created humankind, *'adam,* in the image of God, male and female. In Genesis 2, *'adam,* taken from the earth *('adamah),* is both male and female.

In Gen. 2:22 we are told that God formed woman from *'adam's* rib (or "side"), but she was still made *by God* just as she was in Genesis 1. As woman struggles with her dawning sense of being she must look to God for her identity. When woman looks to Eve she sees the handiwork of God. When woman looks at herself, she must see that same handiwork if she is to have any sense of divine purpose and calling.

So Eve could hear, as she awakened to "being," the voice of God instructing her, along with the man, as to her vocation. The calling began with God's blessing (1:28) on *'adam,* male and female, and followed with some simple instructions for their life together under God.

1. Be fruitful and multiply.
2. Have dominion over every living thing.
3. Eat plants for food.

The first instruction to *'adam* was meant to be a blessing. The arrival of a baby has traditionally been an occasion of much joy for a married couple and for all of their relatives. For some women the time before a baby is born constitutes a spiritual journey as they reflect upon the mystery of creation. The wonder of the developing life in their bodies brings a sense of oneness with God that sometimes causes them to withdraw from other humans into their private mystery.

The instruction to "multiply" is given three times in Genesis: at the creation when there was need to bring forth other human beings (1:28), after the flood when the earth was devastated and barren (9:1,7), and to Jacob when God renewed the covenant with Abraham (35:11).

Now that the earth is replenished with billions of people, the need to multiply in great numbers may not be necessary. In fact, now more than ever, the need for caretaking of the earth, as indicated in God's second instruction to the woman and man, may need to take priority over the multiplying instruction.

But back to the garden. One of the most joy-filled experiences in Eve's dawning consciousness must have been the awareness of her companion in the garden. What a marvel! Here was someone who looked like her and yet was different. Only this one out of all the other creatures in their garden was like her. Perhaps in watching the other creatures they were instructed in some of the mysteries of their own relationship.

In the primeval garden, according to the story, the relationship of woman and man was "very good" (1:31). All was *shalom,* or whole. They were equals, created not from the head or the feet, but from the side of *'adam.*

Now the music in our scenario deepens with foreboding. Into all of this abundance of love and plenty came another voice, the pleasant but disturbing voice of one of the garden's inhabitants. This one was "subtle" (3:1)—and destructive.

Did some of the conversation between Eve and her mate have as its topic that particular tree? Did they wonder about it and the peculiar nature of its fruit? Did they sometimes joke about taking a bite just to see what would happen?

Did the serpent overhear their conversations and simply give them permission to do what they already wanted to do?

The serpent, it seemed, knew something about the trees and about God that they did not know.

We are told that Eve listened to the serpent. Then she looked at the tree and reflected on its possibilities. She studied its qualities and found it appealing to her in many ways. The fruit looked like good food, its appearance delighted her eyes, and it held the promise of wisdom beyond anything she already knew.

So after a brief debate with the serpent she ate some of the forbidden fruit. Then she gave some to her husband and he ate.

And their world crashed around them! The nakedness they had taken for granted as a good and natural condition now appeared shameful. Communication was broken, eye contact was difficult. Instead of being the regal occupants in a peaceful garden, they became furtive fugitives hiding from their Creator and Provider.

A major theme in the account in Genesis 3 is that Eve, prototype and mother of all humanity, is now identified with us in other ways. Her judgment is the judgment we also experience. Maintaining loving and supporting relationships is now a challenge instead of a right. The Bible says that the enmity between men and women both of that time and of ours is a consequence of disobedience to God. Most of us have known the personal alienation and isolation of rifted relationships. Now we all must fight the spirit of rebellion which prevents us from seeing God's original design for our lives.

Eve, whose name means "life" or "life giving," comes through much pain to fulfill her destiny. She is the first woman, mother of us all, including Jesus Christ. Through our common origins we are all brothers and sisters of each other and of our Lord, one in the flesh.

The Summary: Women as Helpers

God did not create human beings to live in isolation. We are social beings who need each other in innumerable ways. God makes that judgment of human nature with the words "It is not good that *'adam* should be alone; I will make a helper fit for him" (2:18).

So much do we need each other, we are told by anthropologists and psychologists, that people get sick and die if they go for long periods without being touched by another human being. Especially important is the cuddling by parents when an infant is small. Experiments have demonstrated that infants will often choose tactile contact over food, given that choice.

In a real sense, man and woman together constitute the culmination of creation. Together they are the ultimate touch in God's created universe, brought into completion by each other.

The meaning of "helper"

The Hebrew word *ezer* has been translated "helper." Some have interpreted "helper" as referring to someone who is of inferior status. A study of the word *ezer* has led to some questioning of that interpretation.

We can uncover meanings just from looking at some usages of the word "helper" *(ezer)* where it occurs in the Scriptures. Let's look at its use in Gen. 2:18 and 2:20. God first created one kind of helper, the animals. Even though *'adam* named them and lived in harmony with them, the animals were not "helpers" fit for *'adam*. As helpers they were inferior. They could not communicate with *'adam* as equals nor provide the kind of companionship necessary for a healthy life.

Looking further into the Scriptures, we discover that *ezer* is also used to describe God as "helper."

Ps. 121:2	My *help* comes from the Lord . . .
Ps. 146:5	Happy is he whose *help* is the God of Jacob
Ps. 33:20	Our soul waits for the Lord:
	He is our *help* and shield.
Deut. 33:7	"Hear, O Lord, the voice of Judah,
	and bring him in to his people.
	With thy hands contend for him,
	and be a *help* against his adversaries."

God is a "helper" superior to humans.

In *God and the Rhetoric of Sexuality* (Fortress, 1978), author and theologian Phyllis Trible sums it up this way. She says that *ezer* is a relational term: it designates a beneficial relationship. Also, it pertains to God, people, and animals. God is the helper superior to humans, the animals are helpers *inferior* to humans, woman is the helper *equal* to man.

The alienation of woman and man

Sin has set man and woman against each other. We are alienated from each other as well as from ourselves. When they covered their nakedness, Adam and Eve gave evidence of complete self-loathing. Now, instead of truly rejoicing in the sight and the touch of each other's bodies, we tend to engage in elaborate rituals to avoid true intimacy. Formal handshakes, ritualized kisses, and orderly chairs and pews keep us from making contact with each other. The body has become the unacceptable symbol of our brokenness.

As a result, sex therapy classes and counselors do a thriving business. People have to learn how to overcome the alienation from their own bodies and therefore from the bodies of their mates in order to be lovers again, enjoying the playfulness and spontaneity of sex.

How then do we account for our highly sexed society? When true and open intimacy cannot be achieved by sexual partners, then sexual performance becomes the goal. Bumper stickers have bragged about doing "it," thus further emphasizing the depersonalization of sex.

The "seed" of the woman

Without the promise of the *seed* tucked away in the crashing words of judgment (3:15) our study would end in despair. But we live in the time of the promise fulfilled. We are once again able to know the kind of relationship Eve experienced with her husband, partner, friend, and lover in the garden.

Jesus is our peace (Eph. 2:14) who has overcome the dividing walls of hostility and made us all one again, bone of bone and flesh of flesh. We know from reading Genesis 1 what it means to be that first *'adam*, male and female created in the image of God. Of course we have to work at achieving and understanding, but even in the garden work was an essential part of life. We work with hope and in the victory of the Cross which has bridged the chasm of alienation and made, out of the two that were separated, one new person.

Eve's story is not an easy one. She is our glory and our shame. If we love Eve, it is because we love ourselves. What we despise in her is that which we despise in ourselves. In her story we find the mixed nature of all human beings: created with great potential, yet struggling with pride and rebelliousness. In her story we also meet a loving God who journeys with people and promises to redeem them again and again.

We cannot forget her. Eve is every one of us. She is woman.

Questions for Reflection

1. In your opinion, which account of creation, Genesis 1 or 2, has most influenced women's understanding of themselves?

2. What is the view of human sexuality in Gen. 2:24-25? How do you account for the idea, held by some, that sex, unless it is for procreation, is sinful even between husband and wife?

3. Read Genesis 3. What human traits do you see in Adam and Eve? Are these true portraits of what human beings are like? Do you see yourself in this story?

4. The writer of Genesis 2 understood clearly that Adam and Eve could *choose* to disobey God. Could there be any human responsibility without that possibility of choice? What evidence of God's love do you find in the story?

5. Think about the so-called battle of the sexes in the light of Gen. 3:16-17. What evidences do you see of the brokenness between men and women in your church and community?

Genesis 12; 21:1-14
(Supplementary texts: Genesis 15:1-7; 16; 17:15-17;
18:1-15; 20)

SARAH

The Setting: God's Call

It is a long journey from Ur of the Chaldeans to Haran in Mesopotamia to Egypt and back to the land of Canaan. Thousands of miles were traveled by Sarah and her husband Abraham in response to God's call.

We actually know a good deal about that world of 4000 years ago. Many scientific expeditions have gone in search of evidence from those ancient cultures. The hot, dry sands of those desert lands have preserved utensils, pots, vases, statues, and the ruins of homes, temples, and public places. The ruins of Ur, the city from which the families of Abraham and Sarah came, first yielded their relics to archeologists in about 1850.

Halfway between the Persian Gulf and the city of Bagdad, the ruins of this flourishing city were discovered buried under the sands of a huge mound. Religion was evidently an important part of the life of Ur. One-third of the north half of the city contained a sacred walled area with a temple dedicated to the worship of the moon god Nanna. The worshipers believed in a life after death, and the royal burial pit revealed the custom of burying servants, soldiers, musicians, and all of their personal attendants with the king and queen. They went willingly, dressed in their finest uniforms and robes, letting their lives be taken with sleeping potions before the grave was filled in.

Writing materials were discovered, demonstrating a complex civilization and educational system. Houses, two stories high around an inner court, were very similar to Iraqi houses today.

Into this environment came the call of the God who is above all deities. How that call came we are not told, but Abraham knew that he had been summoned. Where to, he did not really know. Hebrews 11:8 says he left his own country "not knowing where he was to go." He stopped in Haran after a journey of a thousand miles and many years and there the call came to him again. By this time he was 75 years old, and Sarah, 65.

Finding water in the desert for his large caravan of sheep, oxen, asses, and hundreds of servants and fighting men was difficult for Abraham. Marauding bands of nomads roamed the edges of fertile areas, periodically raiding the sown land.

The Story: The Laughing Princess

(This section is based on the Bible account, scholarly sources, and personal reflection. Let your imagination help you re-create Sarah's story.)

Sarah. The name means "princess." Whether or not she was actually a princess, she had everything that you have been led to believe a princess ought to have. She had money, position, influence, beauty, servants, a loving and prosperous husband—everything.

Everything except a child, that is. And that's the point of Sarah's story.

Children were very important to Sarah. The significance of a child for her went far beyond the normal desires of motherhood. In her world, children meant immortality for a husband. Her world was a patriarchal world which means that in every respect it was a man's world.

Did you notice that even her family line is traced through her husband rather than herself? She is called "the daughter of [Abraham's] father" but not the daughter of [his] mother (Gen. 20:12).

Although the Bible states that Abraham obeyed God, we have to remember that Sarah also left her home and her friends to go with him. Think about what it meant for a woman to leave a city like Ur of the Chaldeans, a center of culture, philosophy, and astronomy, to go wandering in the wilderness and live in tents!

In this patriarchal world only sons could inherit property and carry on the family name. Women were not given a high place in society. When Lot, Abraham's nephew, was in trouble with some men of Sodom, he offered his daughters to them if they would leave him and his male visitors alone. "Behold," he said, "I have two daughters who have not known man; let me bring them out to you, and do to them as you please . . ." (Gen. 19:8).

The world was certainly different for women than for men. Even though Sarah and her husband had a loving relationship, she was not immune to the fate of all women. Whenever they came to a place where the ruler of the region had a harem, Abraham became afraid since Sarah was so beautiful; he knew the owner of the harem would want to add her to his other women. He feared they might kill him to get her.

Scripture records two accounts of Sarah's placement by Abraham in the harem of a powerful man (see Gen. 12:10-20; 20:1-18). In both accounts we get a sense of Sarah's great beauty and worth when Abraham arranges with Sarah to say that she is his sister. Abraham says to her, "This is the kindness you must do for me: at every place to which we come, say of me, 'He is my brother' " (20:13).

Sarah agreed to the arrangement, and her life was put in jeopardy. Yet when the deception was discovered, neither the Pharaoh in one story nor Abimelech in the other reacted as harshly as they might have done. They acted with great tenderness and respect for Sarah. God's protection shielded her from harm because she was important to his plan for a people dedicated to his glory.

In the memory of the writer, God gave evidence of a special relationship with Sarah at the time he made the covenant with her husband. At that time her name was changed from Sarai to Sarah just as Abram was changed to Abraham (see Gen. 17:5,15). Both Sarai and Sarah mean "princess."

Sarah is listed among the great heroes of the faith in Hebrews 11. "By faith," the author of Hebrews writes 20 centuries later, "Sarah herself received power to conceive, even when she was past the age, since she considered him faithful who had promised" (Heb. 11:11).

Why shouldn't Sarah be filled with laughter? God was her refuge and she believed that no harm would come to her as long as she trusted the promise. Joy may have been her daily companion, bubbling up at the thought of the child God had said she would bear. Laughter flows easily from the heart and lips of one who lives under the promises of God. Her joyous laughter might have run over the encampment like a carillon, a reminder to all of the reason for their journeys.

But the young Sarah grew older . . . and older . . . and older. Every month she wondered if this month she would become pregnant. Every month she was disappointed. Her faith faltered; her laughter stilled. Maybe she wouldn't be able to have a child. Some women who could have no children of their own were permitted by the custom of that time to have children through one of their servants. Maybe that's the way God wanted her husband to have an heir, she thought.

"Abraham, I can't have a baby myself. Go to bed with my Egyptian maid, Hagar. Maybe she can bear a child for me" (see Gen. 16:1-2). What a hard thing to say. Not just because she wanted to be the one to bear her beloved's child but because she was openly admitting that God's promise of descendants might not be fulfilled through her. Apparently her husband was beginning to doubt, too, so he obeyed Sarah and the maid became pregnant and gave birth to a son who was named Ishmael.

By this time Sarah's menstrual periods had stopped altogether, and she and Abraham settled down to raising Ishmael as their own son. Hagar and Sarah did not get along very well since Hagar did not hide her contempt for her childless mistress, letting her know in subtle ways that she was not quite the woman Hagar was. Nevertheless, for 14 years Ishmael lived as the rightful son of Abraham.

The "princess" was now a "dowager queen," 89 years old with a 99-year-old husband. And that was the time God chose to fulfill his promise!

Laughter returned to Sarah when she overheard the angelic visitor tell her husband that she was going to become pregnant and give birth to a baby (see Gen. 18:9-15). Laughter, that curious mixture of belief and unbelief, of joy tinged with grief for all those lost years of motherhood, bubbled up again. She could not be discourteous to the stranger called "the Lord" or let him think that she didn't believe him, but one could imagine her struggling to suppress her laughter. How strange to think that she, long past menopause, and her 99-year-old husband would make love again and have a baby!

The dowager queen became a princess full of laughter again. Everything about her was renewed with the fulfillment of God's promise. The Lord rebuked her for laughing, but it was a gentle rebuke and without ill will. In Genesis 20 Scripture records that it was after this incident that Abimelech, king of Gerar, found her so appealing that he took her into his harem, and even when he learned how he had been deceived he sent her away with gifts to vindicate her in the eyes of others.

The child of the promise was born. Laughter was not only restored for Sarah and for Abraham but for all of their offspring throughout the ages. No wonder they named him Isaac, which means "he laughs." As Sarah said, "God has made laughter for me; every one who hears will laugh over me" (Gen. 21:6). The King James version says, "will laugh with me."

The Summary: Women as Mentors

Mentors are persons, usually older than ourselves, who serve as trusted teachers and guides to us. Sarah is a mentor from whom women have learned, and can still learn, valuable lessons.

The gift of laughter and a sense of humor

Of all the creatures God has created, only human beings have the gift of laughter. How delighted parents are when they hear a baby laugh for the first time! They do all kinds of foolish things just to make the baby laugh again. Strangers consider the laughing response of a child a mark of acceptance. The laughter of little children is a sound of pure joy.

As we grow older, experience often dulls our laughter. It becomes tinged with hostility, with scorn, with bitterness, and with derision.

Instead of expressing joy, laughter becomes a poisonous weapon that hurts and kills the spirit. The people laughed at Jesus when he told them that the little girl was not dead but sleeping (see Matt. 9:24). Years before, when Hezekiah had sent out an invitation for people to return to the Lord, the people laughed at the messengers and "mocked them" (2 Chron. 30:10).

Sarah's brand of laughter is echoed by the woman in Proverbs 31:25, "Strength and dignity are her clothing, and she laughs at the time to come." When you know God is with you, why not laugh?

How to treat other women

Whenever women are taught by their culture that they are inferior persons valued only for their sexuality, the tendency is for them to treat other women as inferior also. Sarah yielded to cultural standards when she gave her maid's body to Abraham, using her as an object instead of as a person. Her excuse was that she was simply doing her duty as a wife who was unable to give her husband the child he had to have to make him a worthy man in the eyes of his peers. Her world made her responsible for his having an heir, one way or another. Her mistake was in thinking that infertility—being created with a body which could not conceive babies—was a sin for which she was responsible.

Hagar, on the other hand, suffered from the low self-esteem that always results from being an oppressed person. She was a slave and had no rights over her own body. Then when she became pregnant with the master's child, this became her opportunity to prove to herself that she was a better person than the beautiful, but childless, Sarah.

When we oppress other human beings and use them for our own ends, we can expect them to act out of their need to be accepted as worthy persons. Poor Hagar. Sent out into the desert by Sarah according to the Scriptures. Did she deserve that kind of treatment? Of course not. Can we excuse it because that was the way society was? What makes a society condone the oppression of persons? People are the society. Jesus later said that we are to be in the world "but not of the world" (John 17:14).

Sarah, under her laughter, had to bear the pain caused by yielding to society's pressures. By the faith from which she derived her own sense of self-worth, she knew better. She permitted Hagar to be used and abused and had to live with the knowledge that her lack of faith had caused Hagar and her son to be driven out into the desert.

How to handle physical beauty

While all of us want to look as good as we can, we are well aware of the fact that beauty, inappropriately used by oneself or others, can be a great detriment to women. When we study women of the New Testament, we will be struck by the fact that physical beauty is never mentioned as a desirable attribute for women.

Very few women probably merit the same description as Sarah, that she was "beautiful to behold," but that does not keep them from being seen as beautiful. Even without that description of her, Sarah's gift of laughter and her joy in the Lord would still have attracted others to her. Without that inner joy her beauty would have been empty and her personality one-dimensional. Surely this is what called forth her gentle treatment at the hands of Pharaoh and Abimelech.

Jesus underscored the need for inner beauty when he said, "Do not judge by appearances, but judge with right judgment" (John 7:24). Although women through the centuries have demonstrated their worth in many ways, they still need to resist the devaluation of themselves by advertisements, commercials, and movies that want to define them only by outward appearance and sexual attractiveness.

Sarah was not perfect, but she is a good mentor, a woman whose faith allowed her to accept new possibilities for her life.

Questions for Reflection

1. God made a promise to Sarah and her husband and then waited at least 25 years before keeping it. How does one keep faith during the long years of waiting on the Lord?

2. Reflecting on Hagar's experience, what do you think about today's "surrogate mother"—a young woman who can be hired to have the

fertilized ovum of a married woman who cannot carry a baby implanted into her uterus? What insights might we get from Sarah's experience?

3. Sarah is one of the women who are listed as "matriarchs" in biblical history. Think of some stories of the matriarchs in your family. How have they influenced you?

4. Make a commitment to write a letter to some woman who has been a mentor (a guide or a teacher) in your life. She may have been a relative, teacher, friend, neighbor, or another church member. Tell her what she's meant to you.

3

Genesis 24; 25:19-34; 27:1—28:5

REBEKAH

The Setting: The Place of Meeting

Where and how does one go about meeting one's future spouse? Some people find their mates at work, at church, at the bus stop, at the laundromat, at the grocery store. *Where* one goes to look for a potential life partner often determines the kind of person one marries.

With the divorce rate in our country as high as it is, we can safely say that freedom of choice is not a predictor of marriage success. Young people can go just about anywhere they want to in order to meet and make friends in the hope that one of the friendships will blossom into a permanent relationship.

While in some countries it is still the custom for a young woman to be sheltered from associations with young men until her future husband's identity is made public, that is practically unheard of today in our country. And yet dating, as we practice it, is a fairly recent, 20th-century phenomenon even in the United States.

Probably the closest thing to "matchmaking" that we know of is the "blind date," the arrangement made by a mutual friend for two people to meet. Friends often see similarities in the likes and dislikes of two persons they know and decide that these two would have a great deal in common and would enjoy meeting each other.

The story of Rebekah's marriage to Isaac begins with two old "matchmakers"—Isaac's father Abraham and an old and trusted servant who has no doubt known Isaac all of his life. Their concerns were far from romantic, however. The matter of finding the right woman for Isaac was serious business for Abraham. Sarah, his wife, had died and Abraham was close to death.

The covenant that God had made with Abraham and Sarah, you recall, promised them that their descendants were going to inherit the "land of Canaan" (Gen. 17:8), and those descendants were supposed to come from Isaac (17:19). But Isaac was now 40 years old, not married, and, of course, had no children. Time was moving on.

Where could they find a wife—the *right* wife—for Isaac who, up to this time, had shown no interest in finding a wife? Perhaps he was content to live with his father and mother and felt no need for anyone else. (We know that he was very close to his mother because Gen. 24:67 notes that he needed comfort after his mother's death.) Apparently his father and mother had not been in any hurry to have him leave home either since they had waited so long for this child of laughter and then had come so close to losing him under the sacrificial knife (22:9-14).

Sarah may have had to die before Isaac could find happiness with a wife. You remember the first "rule" for a happy marriage handed down from the beginning? "Therefore a man leaves his father and his mother and cleaves to his wife, and they become one flesh" (Gen. 2:24). Could Sarah and Abraham *ever* have let go of Isaac so that he could "cleave" to a wife? Would they always have wanted part of him to belong to them? Any woman who has married a man who is still dependent on his mother and who turns to her for advice and comfort before he turns to his wife will know only heartache. Isaac had to be ready for a wife and that meant waiting until there was no other alternative but to let go of his most loving parents.

Now the time had come, and Abraham, performing the duty of a father, sent his old and trusted servant to find a wife for his son. His instructions included three stipulations:

1) The woman must not be from the daughters of the Canaanites;

2) She must rather be one of Abraham's relatives from his home country;

3) *She* must be willing to come to Isaac since he *must not* leave this land of promise.

The servant took 10 camels, other servants, and all sorts of gifts, and they began the trek north to Haran and the city of Nahor in Mesopotamia. Eliezer, the old servant, had been well trained by Abraham, knew all about God, and trusted that the God of Abraham and Sarah and Isaac would keep the promise made to them.

When he arrived at his destination near Haran, he stopped to pray, convinced that God had a vested interest in Isaac's wife-to-be. He knew that the city well was the gathering place to which young women would be coming for water.

Wells and watering holes have always been places to meet. In many parts of the world they still serve this function. (In places where public "wells" are no longer common, other kinds of less healthful "watering holes" become places where people go to drink and meet!) Years later Isaac's son Jacob would meet the lovely Rachel at that well, fall in love, and marry her. About 500 years later, Moses, liberator of the Israelites from slavery, would meet his wife at a well in Midian.

Eliezer had good reason to believe that relatives of his dying master drew their water from this very well, so he prayed. In his prayer, he asked God to identify the right girl by her response to his request for a drink of water. If some young woman willingly gave him a drink and then volunteered to bring water for his camels also, Eliezer would accept that as a sign that this particular young woman was God's selection!

This was no small request to make of God or a woman! Wells in that part of the world are often below the surface of the ground, tapping into underground springs. The walk down many rock-hewn steps and back up again carrying a heavy pot of water on one's shoulder was no easy task. How many trips would a woman have to make in order to water ten thirsty camels, each of whom uses about five gallons of water a day and can go up to a month before they need a refill?

The scene was set. The matchmaker had come to the place of meeting. He realized that the future of the covenant rested on one young woman and that she might come to this particular well on that very day.

The Story: Girl of the Promise

(This section is based on the Bible account, insights from scholarly sources, and personal reflection. You are invited to let your imagination make you part of Rebekah's adventure.)

A girl approached. She was carrying a water jar on her shoulder. Eliezer watched as she went down into the well and came back up with her jar filled. Everything proceeded according to the scenario Eliezer had laid before God. She not only gave him a drink "quickly" in response to his request, but, without prompting, she added, "I will draw water for your camels also, until they have done drinking" (Gen. 24:19). Eliezer watched with growing excitement as the young woman made the countless trips down into the well and up again, pouring water into the trough until the thirsty camels had their fill.

Who was this gracious girl? Eliezer remembered Abraham's concern that the chosen one come from among his own relatives.

The Scripture mentions that the "maiden was very fair to look upon" and that she was "a virgin." The narrator might also have added that she was very strong physically because of the endurance contest to which she subjected herself for the old stranger at the well.

Was Rebekah (for that was her name) aware of a more than casual interest on the part of this stranger at the well on that particular day? Her city was on a main trade route from Egypt to Mesopotamia, and perhaps she was used to meeting strange travelers and caravans at the well every day. Even though one has the impression of openheartedness and enthusiasm from this girl, one wonders if she was normally so generous in her offer to water the camels of travelers.

Be that as it may, her freshness and vitality must have delighted the old servant. Eliezer knew Isaac so well. Although his name meant "laughter," Isaac appears serious and restrained in the biblical account, and the young woman presented a refreshing contrast to his more sombre personality. So Eliezer "gazed at her in silence to learn whether the Lord had prospered his journey or not" (Gen. 24:21). Was Rebekah "the woman" whom Abraham had in mind (vv. 5 and 8)? Certainly she was living testimony of his answered prayer for a "sign," and Eliezer repaid her kindness with two gold bracelets and a gold ring (for her nose, we learn later, v. 47).

To his next question about her identity, Rebekah revealed that she was the granddaughter of Abraham's brother Nahor, the daughter of Nahor's son Bethuel, and she invited him to stay with her family.

Then Rebekah ran to tell her mother what had happened while Eliezer, marveling, remained at the well of meeting to worship God for leading him to "the woman" who was, in truth, a relative of Abraham, actually one of the "kindred" Abraham had sent him to find. Laban, Rebekah's brother, found him there and escorted the entire company to their property. We surmise that Laban was probably impressed by the weight of the gold bracelets and the ring (Gen. 24:30) since this was the same Laban who in the next generation made his sister's son Jacob work 14 years in order to win his daughter Rachel in marriage. He was further impressed when Eliezer, recounting the story of his mission, told the family how wealthy Abraham was in "flocks and herds, silver and gold, menservants and maidservants, camels and asses" (v. 35).

Now Rebekah knew why Eliezer had come. If she had had any hint of this at the well, now it was confirmed. Now she knew that at the other end of Eliezer's journey there was a man who was destined to affect the rest of her life. As a woman in her society, she, of course, knew that she had little to say about the choice of a husband. Marriages were arranged by parents, especially by fathers and, in her case, by a brother. That was the way things were done and she would not object.

But thoughts cannot be controlled, and Rebekah must have wondered about this "Isaac" she had never met. Of his wealth there could be no doubt since Eliezer had informed them that Isaac's prosperous father Abraham had given to Isaac "all that he has" (Gen. 24:36). That he was a God-fearing man was evident from Eliezer's own concern for God's leading in the selection of a wife for him. A sense of the rightness of their union must have overwhelmed her when she thought of her own actions at the well as an answer to prayer. In that moment of insight, she knew without a doubt that this man was the one meant for her to marry.

When her mother and brother asked her if she wouldn't stay home with them a little longer rather than complying with the servant's plea that they leave on the return journey at once, she was ready with her answer.

"I will go," was her simple and firm decision (Gen. 24:58). Except for her "nurse" whom we learn later on is named Deborah (35:8), she left everything else behind. Rebekah's attachment to Deborah was so great that when Deborah died, the place near Bethel where she was buried was marked with a special oak tree that was given the name Allon-bacuth, the "oak of weeping."

On the long journey, anticipation of her meeting with Isaac increased. When she saw him in the distance walking and meditating out in the field, she got down from her camel, covered her face with a veil, and went to meet him. He took her into his mother's tent, the marriage was consummated, and Isaac loved Rebekah, his bride of the promise. (The mention in the Hebrew of Sarah's tent is significant indication of Rebekah's place as a covenant ancestress.)

Time passed pleasantly enough for Rebekah but when 10 and then 15 years passed and they still had no children, the time of testing began. Where was the God of the covenant? How would the promise of many descendants for Abraham and Sarah be fulfilled if they remained childless? Not until many prayers had been prayed and 20 years had passed would Rebekah give birth. Her pregnancy was difficult, she was carrying twins and the babies "struggled together within her" to the point where she became depressed and wondered if life was worth living (Gen. 25:22).

Through those long difficult months before the babies were born, Rebekah must have been sustained by the thought of her meeting with Eliezer at the well near her home. She remained vividly aware of the mysterious purpose that had guided that encounter. God had brought her to Abraham and Sarah's promised son as part of some divine plan.

"So she went to inquire of the Lord" in her perplexity over the strange activity in her womb. Instinct told her that something unusual was going on with the growing life in her body. God responded to her prayer.

"Rebekah," we seem to hear God saying, "you have been specially chosen to perform a very important and unique role in my plan for the world I created from my own womb (Deut. 32:18). You are right in sensing that something unusual is going on in your body. Actually, two nations are struggling to be born, the one stronger than the other. I want you to remember what I am about to tell you because *you* will have to be the one who sees that my words are carried out. Only you will remember when the time comes that I have chosen to reverse the usual order of things and that I have chosen the second-born child to take the place normally reserved for the firstborn. In other words, Rebekah, the 'elder shall serve the younger,' and the younger son will be the child of my covenant" (Gen. 25:23). Strange words, indeed, since in a patriarchal society birth order was every-thing for boys; the eldest son received a double portion of the in-heritance (Deut. 21:15-17) and all of the many privileges of the firstborn son.

Through the years of her children's childhood, Rebekah must have observed her two very different boys carefully. Isaac obviously fa-vored Esau, the rough, hairy, active hunter. She favored the quiet, gentle, home-loving Jacob who had emerged last from her womb, the "younger" of the two. She must have marveled at the unfolding prenatal prophecy when Esau sold his birthright to his younger brother for a bowl of lentil soup (Gen. 25:29-34).

Rebekah has often been characterized by biographers as a devious, scheming wife, but was she not carrying out her God-given respon-sibility as preserver of the covenant? If Isaac knew about the words of God to his wife before the birth of their sons, he seemed to have forgotten them or intended to deliberately ignore them. When age came upon him and his eyes could no longer see and he knew that his death was imminent, Rebekah overheard him tell Esau to make him the kind of meat stew he loved, to bring it to him, and he, Isaac, would then give him the formal blessing that passed on his inher-itance and covenant relationship.

Rebekah knew that this must not happen. God's express command must not be violated! We know the rest of the story. Rebekah devised an elaborate scenario to deceive the blind Isaac and to secure the blessing for Jacob, the chosen son. Isaac was deceived; the blessing went to Jacob. She had done what she felt she needed to do. The son chosen by God received the blessing and the elder would "serve the younger."

We can judge Rebekah for not having faith that God would fulfill the promise without her help, but how does one know how much depends on God alone and how much depends on the one who has been given the vision? Had not Sarah and Abraham picked a surrogate mother because they felt God needed help with the promise? How did Rebekah know if there was any other method by which God would keep the promise given to her? Was there a "Plan B" ready if "Plan A" failed for want of her action? We certainly cannot imagine another course of action in view of Isaac's determination to give his favorite son Esau the paternal blessing.

Rebekah, the fair, the strong, the chosen, had come a long way from the maiden at the well outside her city. The meeting that long-ago time *seemed* to be a matter of divine destiny; now she knew why.

The Summary: Women as Decision Makers

The particular quality in Rebekah that made her an ideal choice for marriage with Isaac may have been her decisiveness. She did not hesitate when asked to leave her home with Eliezer. The simple statement "I will go" expressed strength and certainty. We learn through these few words that, having once committed herself to a course of action, Rebekah let nothing stand in her way.

Isaac needed a wife of the purposeful nature demonstrated by Rebekah. Our impression of Isaac is that of a man from whom no decision making was ever demanded. His parents had made all of his decisions for him. He was peaceloving and nonviolent by nature. Like his father before him, he even tried to avoid possible violence against himself by pretending that his lovely wife was his sister (Gen. 26:6-11).

When the herdsmen of Gerar twice demanded that he give up the wells he had patiently reclaimed from a state of disrepair, Isaac moved on to another grazing site without protest rather than fight with them (Gen. 26:17-22). In a land without much water, surrendering a productive well is a generous but almost unheard of act of peace making.

Isaac's pacific and kind nature probably endeared him to Rebekah, but when it came to keeping the covenant, she knew that no surrender could be permitted. She could not allow him to give the covenant inheritance and blessing to the wrong son no matter how much he loved him. If God had a second plan, she did not know what that was, but she did know that the plan revealed to her before the birth of her children required son Jacob to be the inheritor.

Once more, Rebekah did not hesitate. Having made up her mind to deceive Isaac and to secure the promised blessing for Jacob, she did not vacillate. When Jacob revealed his own fear that his father would see through the scheme and bring a curse upon him, Rebekah accepted the responsibility for her actions, "Upon me be your curse, my son; only obey my word, and go . . ." (Gen. 27:13).

The same unhesitating, fearless commitment to an unknown future marks all of Rebekah's actions. She takes responsibility for all of her decisions. "I will go . . ." rings down the years of her life as a challenge to uncertainty.

Rebekah is the foremother of all of the young women who have made the decision to leave their homelands to face unknown tomorrows in foreign lands with men who are practically strangers to them. They sailed many months across vast oceans, endured the hardships of long, lonely treks over strange continents, knowing not where they were going but trusting the decisions they made in answer to prayer and their commitment to God. Sometimes disappointment was their lot, but for many of our foremothers, good marriages and enduring satisfaction awaited them.

Rebekah, the decision maker, was the perfect partner for Isaac. Even though sociologists and psychologists tell us that we could probably be suitably mated with any one of several thousand persons of the opposite sex, women and men who look to God for help with their life choices usually feel that the person they married was uniquely designed for them. No one can convince them otherwise. Rebekah seemed to have no doubt about her life choices when she looked at the circumstances surrounding her meeting with Isaac.

Seeing the "signs" of God's guidance in the events of our lives and then responding with our human understanding to those signs makes decision making easy for women who trust in God.

Questions for Reflection

1. It's possible that Abraham had Rebekah in mind when he sent his servant back to his kindred. If his use of the definite article in

his words *"the woman"* indicates that, what do you think he remembered about his brother that made him assume that his granddaughter would be right for Isaac?

2. Why do you suppose that Rebekah showed no fear of the strangers at the well? How would you react to this incident if Rebekah were your sister or daughter?

3. If arranged marriages are the rule in most parts of the world, what's the probability that they could be arranged here with the possible outcome of more lasting unions?

4. There are not many instances in the Scripture of women being given the opportunity to make the kind of independent decision that Rebekah's family allowed her to make. What might have accounted for the freedom they gave her?

4

Exodus 15:19-21; Numbers 12
(Supplementary texts: Exodus 1:1-22; 2:1-10; Micah 6:4)

MIRIAM

The Setting: A Period of Oppression

While our story is about Miriam and not about the exodus itself, the two stories are inseparable. The exodus is the story of her people, their bondage in Egypt, and their great deliverance under God's mighty hand.

How well we know the story. Joseph, Israel's ancestor, was sold into slavery by his brothers and brought to Egypt. Because of the favor he found with the pharaoh who ruled Egypt at that time, he was permitted to rescue his family from starvation when famine hit the land in which they lived.

Some 400 years after Joseph died, the original 70 male relatives and their families had grown into a large minority group in the land of Egypt (see Gen. 46:8-27 for a list of their names). When a new pharaoh came into power who did not remember the greatness of Joseph, the people of Israel were seen as a political threat. It was this pharaoh who decided that they had to be restricted in their growth and productivity.

First of all he conscripted the Israelites into labor battalions and set them to hard work building treasure cities. Egyptian taskmasters were the supervisors, but the foremen were chosen from the Israelites.

The history of oppression is always the same. The oppressed are valued as an economic resource but feared as a political power or as a threat to the cultural dominance of the oppressor. The oppressed are therefore exploited as a work force but restricted in political and cultural power.

All the hard labor did not prove to be a deterrent to the growth in numbers of the Hebrews. In fact they seemed to thrive; they produced more children, and their growth rate exceeded that of the Egyptians.

Once set on this cruel course the succeeding pharaohs pushed ahead with even more oppressive measures. The next order went out to kill all boys at birth. The midwives who attended the Hebrew women were given instructions to attend the birthstools and to immediately kill all male babies but to let the daughters live. Because the midwives were God-fearing women, they disobeyed, telling the pharaoh that the Hebrew women delivered their babies faster than the Egyptian women so that the midwives got to them after their babies were born!

The Bible history makes the pharaoh appear extremely stupid to believe this ridiculous story. Yet this history fits admirably with our understanding of the dynamics of oppression. The fear that often motivates slavemasters is rooted in their distorted perception of the powers of the enslaved group. The more vigorous and potent they perceive the oppressed to be, the more harshly they apply restrictive measures.

In another phase of the oppression the pharaoh ordered all Hebrew male babies to be thrown into the Nile.

The period of oppression for the Hebrews living in Egypt lasted perhaps 300 years, from the 16th through the 13th centuries B.C. The history of Egypt during this period is a complex one, and historians continually assess the evidence of archeology and the biblical account. The latest evidence suggests the exodus occurred under the reign of the pharaoh Rameses II, shortly after 1290 B.C. Egypt was at this time a great world power, its wealth and influence still apparent in the remarkable treasures and temples that have survived to this day.

Our study of the Scripture reminds us that the revelation of God does not take place in some "religious" sphere unrelated to reality, but that God is made known in the concrete events of human history. While the escape of one minority group of people may not have been viewed by the Egyptians as a particularly significant event, the Bible's historian sees it as it is—the intervention of God on behalf of a special people.

The exodus, under the leadership of Moses, Miriam, and Aaron, is really God's story, not their story. It may well be the story of redemption itself. We must view it that way because that's the way the people of Israel viewed the exodus event (see Deut. 26:5-9).

We will not be studying the events prior to the exodus as such because our concern is with Miriam rather than with Moses. You might want to read Exodus Chapters 1–15 as a continuous story before reading the following story.

The Story: The Big Sister

(This section is based on the Bible account, insights from scholarly sources, and personal reflection. You are challenged to let your imagination make you part of the story of Miriam, too.)

What a remarkable child, Miriam! Born into a family of slaves, she learned very early in life how to survive in an alien country. Like all oppressed people she learned to know how the minds of the oppressors worked, what their habits were, and even how they could be manipulated. Survival depends on such knowledge when you yourself have no power.

So when her baby brother was born and survived the midwife's "birthstool" (Exod. 1:16), Miriam and her mother managed to keep the baby hidden from the authorities for three months. The ruling of the pharaoh that only male babies had to be killed indicates that girls were not thought to be worth much at that time; yet how fortunate Moses was that he had a big sister, one who could help her mother hide him and outwit the Egyptians!

Miriam was a true daughter of her mother, Jochebed. That remarkable mother is mentioned by name only twice in Scripture (Exod. 6:20; Num. 26:59). Perhaps her influence is most significantly noticed in her daughter, since her sons had all the opportunities open to capable men both in that day and now.

Miriam would have been an outstanding woman in any age, but living as she did during that period in history and under conditions of oppression, she shone with radiance among all of the women chosen by God for leadership throughout the ages.

When they could no longer hide the growing, noisier, and more active baby, Miriam and her mother arranged a way not only to save him but to gain an advantage for their whole family. Perhaps there was no thought of that baby's future significance for the people of Israel, but then again since the Bible names Miriam as the first woman prophet, who knows? (*Prophet* is a neutral word applicable to both men and women. To add "ess" is not necessary for Miriam.)

During the time of Joseph, the Egyptian royal family had lived in the delta region. When the "king who did not know Joseph" conquered the former dynasty, the capital was moved to Thebes. History tells us that the Egyptian court was moved back to the delta area in the last quarter of the 14th century B.C. in order that the government might be in a better position to control the empire.

This change in location of the pharaoh's residence accounts for the fact that the Egyptian princess went down to the river to bathe in an area not far from the Hebrew colony where Miriam lived. Of course Miriam and all the other children knew that. The whereabouts and habits of the royal family were not only of great general interest, but Miriam's family had to be especially aware in order to save the baby. The family plan for Moses' salvation rested on Miriam. She was the only one insignificant enough in the eyes of the Egyptians to be entrusted with the all-important encounter with the royal princess. The boy Aaron, the Levite father, or a protective mother could be too easily suspected of a plot.

The little girl placed the baby's basket in the reeds along the riverbank at exactly the place where she knew the princess would come but where the attendants could not see it. You know the rest of the story well. Jewish tradition adds that the princess lifted the basket herself since the maids feared the pharaoh's edict.

The poise of the child Miriam amazes the reader. She never betrayed her relationship with the baby or indicated in any way that the Hebrew nurse she offered to bring was the baby's mother. If the princess suspected, she gave no indication.

Was Miriam a born leader or a chosen leader? Or both? She apparently grew up knowing that she was different from the women around her. In a day when marriage was the vocational destiny for women in Israel, she never did marry. She may have believed that her destiny lay with the family of Israel rather than with a husband and children of her own. How many missionaries, teachers, doctors, social workers, and nuns have chosen the single life in order to give themselves without distraction to their calling? Miriam appears to have been such a woman.

When we first meet the adult Miriam she is absorbed in her leadership role in the liberation of her people. She is singing and dancing with total abandon, leading the women of Israel in a song of praise to the God who has saved them. She accompanies herself with the tambourine in a spontaneous outpouring of praise:

Sing to the Lord, for he has triumphed gloriously,
the horse and his rider he has thrown into the sea! (Exod. 15:21).

Dr. Bernhard Anderson, in his book *Understanding the Old Testament,* says that this couplet is one of the oldest pieces of poetry in the Old Testament, and in all probability it originated during the very event it celebrates. It was later incorporated into the liturgical Song of Moses and Miriam.

Miriam's song culminates the exodus as it ends with the closing of the waters over the soldiers of the pharaoh. Then comes the long trek in the wilderness.

How wearying that journey was for the liberated Israelites! It was marked with grumbling, discontent, and rebellion against the leadership. The day came when even Miriam and Aaron joined in the criticism of their brother. The three of them had been a team, sharing ideas and making plans together for the people entrusted to their leadership. Then Moses made a significant personal decision, apparently without consulting his brother and sister. He married a Cushite, or Ethiopian, woman.

Resentment may have been building in Miriam and Aaron for some time. Blowups like the one they expressed result from an accumulation of feelings rather than one isolated event. They did as much work and suffered as much hardship as Moses but he seemed to get all the glory. God always intervened in *his* behalf. What about *them?* What credit were *they* getting?

Ah, Miriam, we would like to think of you as a superwoman but you are just like the rest of us—human. And Aaron was just as petty as you. But understanding deserts us when we consider your punishment. Why the unequal penalty imposed on you? Because we cannot doubt the goodness and justice of God, we must suppose that you were the leader in the rebellion and Aaron your follower.

Miriam, the prophet, became a leper. Let it be said to Aaron's credit that he did not lay all the blame on his sister but assumed responsibility with her for having "done foolishly and . . . sinned" (Num. 12:11). The brothers remembered the goodness of their sister toward them and intervened with the Lord on her behalf.

Miriam was healed but lost her position of leadership. Scripture does not mention her again until Num. 20:1, which records her death at Kadesh. The historian of a later date remembers her leadership and includes her as the only woman in his list of the descendants of Levi (1 Chron. 6:1-15, see v. 3). Contemporary Jewish women honor her as one of their foremothers and as a leader of women. She is seen as the one who, through her dancing and singing, inspired the Israelites to escape, to cross the Red Sea.

The Summary: Women as Liberators

Miriam stands in sharp contrast to the traditional concept of woman's role. History calls forth women like Miriam from what might otherwise be routine and passive participation in society to become active change agents. Centuries of conditioning as nurturers in the role of mothers have made many women extremely sensitive to injustice and the hurts of people.

Church sociologist Lyle Schaller wrote in his book *Women as Pastors* that denominations with the greatest number of ordained women tend to have a greater sensitivity to the oppressed. Even before women were permitted ordination, they had a long history of caring for the outcasts of society.

Women as monastics

The idea of women as religious leaders has been a highly controversial one. Since the care of home and family has made its primary demands upon mothers rather than fathers, married women have often been denied leadership roles.

When asceticism (the renunciation of social life for solitude and self-denial) rose as a dominating influence in the Christian church of the fourth century A.D., many women flocked to God's call rather than the traditional roles of women in society.

"Women religious"

From this period almost until the present time women who wanted to fulfill a religious calling have had to dedicate themselves to the single, celibate life. Flourishing communities of women religious (members of religious orders) were established in the Middle Ages.

In the period of Reformation and Counter-Reformation, women religious entered more into the active life of society, but still had to deny themselves marriage and motherhood in order to do so. Sometimes their vows let them live at home, sometimes they stayed in communities from which they went out to nurse and teach. Lutheran "deaconesses," although allowed to marry, followed in this tradition, and active communities continue to this day. (Read *Bright Valley of Love* by Edna Hong for a moving account of their work in Germany.)

Women as reformers

Between 1795 and 1835, during a period of American religious reform known as the Second Great Awakening, the energies of Protestant women were claimed as volunteers. Many women came out of their homes for the first time to work among the poor, the illiterate, and the dispossessed. Their eyes opened to the desperate needs around them, and the organization of women's societies to support missionaries around the world and workers in their own communities increased.

By 1838 there were approximately 473 "female moral reform societies" out of New England and New York which, according to

Dorothy C. Bass, "sought to reclaim prostitutes, educate girls to the wiles of seducers, and, most grandly, to create 'a union of sentiment and effort among . . . virtuous females from Maine to Alabama.' "

Women as abolitionists

It was natural that women should be shocked by slavery's denial of marriage rights for slaves and the enforced separation of husbands and wives, parents and children. However, as female abolitionists began to speak out against racism and profit, the clergy sometimes insisted that this was not their proper sphere of activity. Quaker women like Sarah and Angelina Grimke could not be deterred and were especially outspoken and powerful in their advocacy of human rights.

Women today

Now women are involved in leadership positions in all areas of civic and church life. Partnership is still the ideal as it was for Miriam and her brothers, men and women working side by side to free the people of our world from all manner of bondage. Now in many places, the opportunities for women to serve God in leadership positions have been broadened.

Questions for Reflection

1. Read Exodus 1:1-14. Do you see any similarities between the position of the Israelites in Egypt and minority groups in our country? Who might represent the forces of Pharaoh today?

2. Read Exodus 1:15-22. What role did the women of Israel play in the liberation of their people? Where did they get the courage necessary to defy the authorities?

3. Some Bible scholars think that Miriam's song was a spontaneous response to the crossing of the sea and that Moses incorporated it into his longer poem when the anniversary was remembered later. Why might Miriam's original contribution have been overlooked?

4. Reflect on the unequal punishments given to Aaron and Miriam in Numbers 12. Do you think the position of women in a patriarchal society might have anything to do with it? How does the writer see God's role in Miriam's punishment?

5

Judges 4 and 5
(Supplementary texts: 2 Kings 22:14-20)

DEBORAH

The Setting: The Time of the Judges

The people of Israel entered their promised land with a blast of trumpets at Jericho, and Joshua led the wilderness wanderers into the land of Canaan. No welcome mats, red carpets, bright balloons, or banners greeted them. Instead, they faced a long and bloody struggle for possession of the land.

Both the book of Joshua and the book of Judges tell the story of that conquest. Joshua presents a picture of a unified people of Israel systematically carrying on a united campaign under Joshua's leadership. The book of Judges gives what is perhaps a more realistic account of separate Israelite tribes waging battles with hostile neighboring tribes for the territory allotted to each of them.

An even more terrifying enemy awaited them in the religion of the Canaanites. The worship of Baal caused the people of Yahweh to be afraid, but the long-suffering love of God rescued them time and again. A cycle established itself, and it went like this:

- faithfulness under a God-chosen leader;
- apostasy to the Baals after the leader's death;
- Yahweh's judgment: oppression by an enemy;
- the people's cry for deliverance;
- another judge/deliverer is sent by Yahweh in answer;
- faithfulness under another chosen leader;
- apostasy after the leader's death;
- and the cycle repeats itself (see Judg. 2:11-19).

The deliverers raised up by God to lead the Israelites out of their oppressions are referred to as "judges." The verb "judged" in place of the title "judge" is used to refer to eight of the twelve leaders whose deeds are recorded in the book. Again, they were not primarily legal consultants or persons who gave judicial opinions but were military leaders who delivered Israel from its enemies. Only in Deborah's case in the book of Judges is the role of judicial arbitration highlighted with the statement that "the people of Israel came up to her for judgment" (4:5).

At the advice of his father-in-law Jethro, Moses had delegated some of his growing load of leadership responsibilities to "judges." They functioned as civil servants having varying degrees of responsibility as "rulers of thousands, of hundreds, of fifties, and of tens" (Exod. 18:18-23). Although arbitration in matters of dispute was their primary task, their function as rulers probably came into greater focus when the military needs of Israel in the land of Canaan called that forth.

Twelve judges are named, six "major" and six "minor." In Ruth 1:1 we are told that her story takes place during "the days when the judges ruled" in the 12th and 11th centuries B.C. Actually, the successive reigns of the judges covered 410 years, marked by an almost artificial structuring of time into periods of oppression and peace. The frequent use of 40, 80, and 20 years may mean one, two, or one-half generation(s).

Whether or not we can make the time line of Judges fit that of the rest of biblical or historical evidence is irrelevant to this study. What we are concerned with is what was happening to Israel's faith during the time of the judges.

In the wilderness, the Israelites had been wanderers, living day to day by the providence of God. Manna had been their basic food. Flocks and herds had supplemented their needs in the wilderness for meat, clothing, and sacrifice. In the land of promise, however, they were confronted with people sophisticated in agriculture. Unless they could make nature yield up the secrets of seedtime and harvest in the same way as the inhabitants of Canaan did, their very survival was threatened. As settled people, contained within the boundaries of their tribal geography, they had to learn how to make the land produce food to replace the manna which had fallen from heaven in the wilderness.

Baal, the god of fertility, was the answer, said the Canaanites. Baal and his wife Asheroth (or we should say "the *baals* and their wives the asheroth" because there were many local *baals* and asheroth) were responsible for the yearly fertility of the land, according to the faith of the Canaanites. The abundant harvests were the result of the sexual activity of these gods and goddesses. Through their religious worship and sexual rituals the farmers tried to control and appease the gods to insure abundant productivity.

The Israelites, like many people who have pondered the yearly cycle of winter and spring, of seedtime and rains, of sprouting and harvest, began to wonder if their Yahweh was indeed a god of agriculture as well as the shepherd of wandering flocks of sheep. As long as a strong prophetic leader kept their theology straight, they understood Yahweh as a god above all human manipulation, a sovereign Lord to whom they were to remain loyal, a god not subject to ritual "magic." But when the leader died, the Israelites looked at the worshipers of Baal and Asheroth, believing that if they too could imitate the sexual activity of the gods they could release magic powers upon the land to increase its productivity. They incorporated some of these beliefs and activities into their worship of Yahweh (Judg. 3:7) and "did what was evil in the sight of the Lord, forgetting the Lord their God, and serving the Baals and the Asheroth."

The nations of Canaan—the Sidonians, the Hivites, the Hittites, the Amorites, the Perizzites, and the Jebusites—were allowed to dwell among the tribes of Israel for "the testing of Israel, to know whether Israel would obey the commandments of the Lord" (3:4). Over and over again, Israel failed the test.

Without the faithfulness of God, Israel would have been lost and perhaps along with it God's promised salvation. Fortunately, God did not permit their apostasy to succeed. Their oppression under the tribes of Canaan increased and they lived as slaves under them (Judg. 3:8,14; and 4:2).

The oppression was a sign of God's love because it caused the people to cry out to the God who had led them out of bondage in Egypt to once again become their savior. God's answer to their cry in each case was to raise up a leader who would once again speak the word of the Lord to them and bring them out of their distress.

The Story: The Commander-in-Chief

(This section is based on the Bible account, scholarly sources, and personal reflection. You are challenged to let your imagination re-create your sister in the faith, the prophet Deborah.)

Deborah was chosen by Yahweh to free the people from the oppressor. Before her, Othniel had prevailed over Cushan-rishathaim, king of Mesopotamia, Ehud had led the young people to victory over the Moabites, and Shamgar delivered Israel from the Philistines.

Now a woman was chosen as judge over Israel. Her authority as a charismatic leader gifted with wisdom and prophetic insights was acknowledged as the people of Israel came to her for judgment where she sat under a palm tree—"the palm of Deborah between Ramah and Bethel in the hill country of Ephraim" (Judg. 4:5). As was mentioned before, only Deborah of all those who judged Israel is identified as having the function of judicial decision or arbitration. Try to imagine this woman, gifted with great wisdom and insight, sitting patiently under her special tree, listening to tales of heartbreak, anger, depression, loss, and abuse, and gently counseling the distressed.

Then hear the Lord speaking to her and telling her that the time had come to lead the people into battle.

Sisera, the Canaanite general against whom Deborah was asked to lead the Israelites, had at his command 900 chariots of iron and all the men it took to ride them and to fight alongside them. He represented a powerful coalition of Canaanite tribes.

At stake in the battle was control over the Valley of Jezreel, through which ran the main commercial route from Egypt to Mesopotamia. The Israelites had managed to hold the hill country, but the fertile plains and the trade routes belonged to the Canaanites. The fortress of Megiddo stood guard over the valley, effectively blocking the economic development of Israel. Near this fortress the armies of Canaan and Israel met in battle (Judg. 5:19), on the same plain in which the book of Revelation says that the last great battle on earth will be fought (Rev. 16:16), the battle of Armageddon ("hill of Megiddo").

In this political and economic setting the word of the Lord came to Deborah. She was a prophet and as the current judge and ruler she was also in the position of commander-in-chief of the armies, a military position. As a prophet she knew that the Lord required faithfulness on the part of the people and that they had gone after false gods (Judg. 4:1). Deborah's spirit must have been distressed as she listened day after day to the sins of God's people and heard their cries for deliverance.

Would Deborah rather have accomplished the deliverance of the people by peaceful means? We will never know, of course, because the message that she gave to her military commander Barak, was this: "The Lord, the God of Israel, commands you, 'Go, gather your men at Mount Tabor, taking 10,000 from the tribe of Naphtali and the tribe of Zebulun. And I will draw out Sisera, the general of Jabin's army, to meet you by the river Kishon with his chariots and his troops; and I will give him into your hand' " (Judg. 4:6-7).

The marvelous assurance with which she speaks the word of the Lord! She does not preface her words with "it seems to me" or "I think God wants you to gather your men at Mount Tabor," nor did she say, "I'll have to check this out with my husband or with a priest." Deborah was so attuned to the Spirit of God that she knew without a doubt what the Word of the Lord was. How did she know? All we know is that she *knew* and she spoke that which she knew.

And the people trusted that word which came through her. Even the other tribes of Israel came to do her bidding (Judg. 5:13-18). Fainthearted Barak said he would go only if Deborah came with him (4:8). People always seem to know when they hear a genuine word from the Lord. False prophets cannot deceive for long. So when Deborah, God's prophet, spoke, the people listened and obeyed.

Our thoughts cannot help but stray to Deborah's husband, Lappidoth, as she marches off to do battle against 900 chariots of iron and thousands of troops. Did he worry? Did he stand in awe of this woman to whom he was married? Had he learned to trust her judgment and to support her in her decisions? We thank God for Lappidoth for not interfering with Deborah's vocation. How enriched our own sense of calling is because of her commitment and his love.

The story of the battle at Megiddo has two versions, one prose (Judges 4) and the other poetry (Judges 5), a style which is unique in the book of Judges. Archeological discoveries at the fortress of Megiddo have produced evidence for dating the battle and the "song" recounting it in the latter part of the 12th century B.C. This dating makes the song of Deborah in Chapter 5 one of the oldest pieces of poetry in the Old Testament. It represents an eyewitness account, whereas the prose version was written later.

Jael, another remarkable woman, figures largely in the victory over the Canaanites. She is the woman whom Deborah foresees when she tells Barak that "the road on which you are going will not lead to your glory, for the Lord will sell Sisera into the hand of a woman" (Judg. 4:9). She comes into the story when the battle has taken a decisive turn for the worse for the Canaanites.

The rains came and the iron chariots sank into the muds caused by the overflowing river Kishon. Sisera got away on foot and entered the tent of Jael, the wife of Heber, something that men were not permitted to do. Sisera took advantage of the fact that Jael's husband was at peace with the Canaanite king, Jabin.

Jael extended hospitality to him with the customary bowl of sour milk curds. At this point the prose and poetry versions differ, one saying that she killed him in his sleep, the other that she killed him when he unguardedly had his head down drinking the curds. In either case her hand, skilled at driving tent pegs into the ground through many nomadic journeys, drove the tent peg through his head and killed Sisera. While the prose version (Judg. 4:17-22) presents Jael as a treacherous killer taking advantage of a sleeping man, the earlier poetic account (5:24-27) praises her as the "most blessed of women" (5:24). You will have to decide for yourself what you think about her while remembering that we often judge women on standards different from those on which men are judged. Would it make a difference in your thinking if Jael's husband had killed Sisera instead?

Deborah's spirituality is nowhere more evident than in the song of Chapter 5. She had had to encourage Barak every step of the way into battle: "Up! For this is the day in which the Lord has given Sisera into your hand. Does not the Lord go out before you?" (Judg.

4:14). Yet she shared the song of praise to God with him. God is the One who is given the glory for the victory. It was the Lord who sent the rain that made the river overflow, "from heaven fought the stars, from their courses they fought against Sisera" (5:20)

The validation of Deborah's leadership is found in the sentence at the end of Chapter 5, "And the land had rest for 40 years."

The Summary: Women as Prophets

Our age calls for prophets who will speak out against war and destruction. With the life and teachings of Jesus informing our understanding of peace and peacemaking, Deborah's calling as prophet takes precedence for us over her role as military leader.

No one decides that he or she is going to be a prophet. Prophets are called into being by God and often over their protests. To prophets is given the difficult task of reminding people that God is present, seeing their evil deeds and their apostasy and calling them to repentance and change of life, and speaking a word of God, whether judgment or grace.

Although foretelling is not their primary function, prophets often are given glimpses into future events as warnings or promises to the people of God. Generally, prophets have not been popular people during their lifetimes. If anyone desires to be a prophet let her consider the words of Hebrews 11:36-38, "They were stoned, they were sawn in two, they were killed with the sword; . . . destitute, afflicted, ill-treated. . . ."

Once chosen, prophets are blessed (or cursed) with knowledge that others do not have. They see clearly what is happening in historical events and where these events will lead if the word of the Lord is not heard and obeyed.

A woman by the name of Huldah is listed in the Old Testament as a prophet. In the New Testament, Anna is called a prophet (Luke 2:36) and the four daughters of Philip the Evangelist were said to have prophetic gifts (Acts 21:9). Huldah was so well-known for her prophetic wisdom that, when the king Josiah wanted a word from the Lord about the book of the law that had been found, the high priest Hilkiah knew exactly where to go (2 Kings 22:14). He went to consult with Huldah whose husband was the keeper of the wardrobe and who lived in the Second Quarter in Jerusalem.

As a result of Huldah's word from the Lord, Josiah repented of the evil into which his people had fallen as they burned incense to other gods. Sweeping reforms were made by Josiah in Judah. The matter of fulfillment of future predictions is called into question when Huldah predicts a peaceful death for Josiah if he does what is right in God's eyes. Instead, Josiah dies at the hands of Pharaoh Neco at Megiddo (2 Kings 23:29). But the women prophets of the Old Testament bear witness to the fact that God chooses people to speak the word of prophecy regardless of sex, age, race, or conditions of life, even as the promise was given to Joel (Joel 2:28-29).

Among the prophets of the present age, a woman like Rachel Carson stands out prominently. In her book *Silent Spring,* with prophetic insight and courage she called the attention of the nation to what was happening to the environment through the use of pesticides and the accumulation of pollutants.

Dr. Helen Caldicott has been waging a vigorous battle against the nuclear arms race and its potential for the destruction of the earth and its inhabitants.

When God reveals to anyone where evil deeds and disregard for God's creation and other humans are leading, then that person must heed the prophetic call. Ezekiel warns, "Son of man, I have made you a watchman for the house of Israel; whenever you hear a word from my mouth, you shall give them warning from me" (Ezek. 3:17).

For most of us our insights come from the Scripture and our warnings to others come out of our own closeness to that Word. If we are truly attuned to the voice of the Lord, then people will know and come to be instructed even as they came to Deborah sitting under her palm tree and to Huldah in her home in the Second Quarter of Jerusalem.

Questions for Reflection

1. Read Judg. 4:4-9. What characteristics did Deborah have that qualified her to be selected by God as a judge in Israel? How do you feel about her as God's chosen leader?

2. Note the difference in the role of a judge in ancient Israel compared to a judge in our present judicial system.

3. How did you feel when you read the story of Jael and Sisera? Can you sense any feeling on the part of the writers? (Read in Judg. 3:15-23 the story of the judge who ruled before Deborah.) What happens to people when violence is normalized and deceitfulness becomes a virtue? Can you think of examples in our own time?

4. Although we don't know whether Deborah had children, she is called "a mother in Israel" (Judg. 5:7). What might this mean? Recall some "mothers in Israel" you have known in your life.

5. Both Deborah and Huldah were married. Discuss the relationship a man might have with a wife who is a prophet. What might he feel?

RUTH

The Setting: The Sojourn in Moab

Do you remember what the "days when the judges ruled" were like? In Session 5 we followed the military leader, Deborah, into a bloody and murderous battle while she was serving as a judge in Israel. Other judges in Israel had equally bloody careers. For example, there was left-handed Ehud who tricked his fat enemy, the king of Moab, by pretending to have a message from God, while thrusting his sword into the king's belly with his unsuspected left hand. The fat swallowed the blade and the enemy was vanquished! (see Judg. 3:12-30). There was Jephthah who vowed to make a sacrifice to God for helping him conquer the Ammonites "with a very great slaughter," and the sacrifice was the life of his only daughter (see Judg. 11:29-40). And then there was Samson who burned all the fields of the Philistines and 300 foxes by tying torches to the tails of the animals and turning them loose in the fields, causing the Philistines to burn to death his wife and father-in-law (see Judg. 15:1-8).

Yet the tender story of Ruth takes place during the time of the judges. Reading the book of Ruth after reading Judges is like coming upon a shining pearl in the mud of a war-torn battlefield. But then, if we compressed 350 years of U.S. history into one book the size of Judges, our history might appear to be only violence, too. Still, in the midst of all the violence, we continue our lives: we marry, we give birth, we get sick, our loved ones die, we sorrow and mourn but go on living. It is entirely possible, then, that the events in the book of Ruth occurred during one of the violent periods of the rule of the judges.

Then again, the story may have its setting during one of those periods when the "land had rest for 40 (or 80) years" (Judg. 3:11,30). The events cover one generation of one family, years that might have encompassed periods of both depression and prosperity. In the days before modern irrigation, the Palestinian harvests depended on "the autumn rain and the spring rain" (Jer. 5:24). The Lord had warned that the promised land had no Nile river watering it but was a land "which drinks water by the rain from heaven" (Deut. 11:11). Without rain, gardens remained barren, and a few rainless years could produce famine and economic hardship.

The family that the book of Ruth tells about is an ordinary family affected, as is every family, by the weather, the economic situation, and international conflict. Like millions of other families throughout history they migrated to an alien land in search of better living conditions for themselves and their children. They left their hometown, the village of Bethlehem in Judea, about six miles south of Jerusalem. Conditions must have been extremely bad to make Elimelech and Naomi take their two sons, Mahlon and Chilion, to a foreign land, leaving behind the property that was their inheritance in their homeland.

Into the desert they went, south and east around the Dead Sea into the land of Moab. The land was a rolling plateau about 4300 feet above the Dead Sea with a steep descent to its shores on the west. In between the cliffs and the eastern desert runs a narrow, well-watered strip that produces good grain crops. Apparently at certain times there were friendly relations between Moab and Israel, and people from both countries crossed the border with ease.

While the story takes place during the period of the judges, there are indications that it was actually written down much later. For instance, in Chapter 4 verse 7 reference is made to the exchange of a sandal in confirmation of a business transaction as being "the custom in former times in Israel." At the time of writing, the custom was apparently obsolete.

Why was this delightful story, told and retold through the generations, written down at a later period? Reason can probably be found in the fact that when Nehemiah and Ezra rebuilt Jerusalem and its temple after the Babylonian captivity and exile, they instituted nationalistic reforms including an attempt to annul all mixed marriages (Neh. 13:23-25). Ruth's foreignness is pointed to throughout the book (1:4,22; 2:2,6,10,21; 4:5,10), and the genealogy at the end stresses the fact that this "foreigner" was one of the ancestors of the great King David. As *The Interpreter's Bible* points out in its introduction to the book of Ruth, the story is a plea for the inclusion of foreigners in the assembly of Israel. It denies the force of Deut. 23:3, and supports Isa. 56:1-8 against the attitude of Ezra and Nehemiah.

While Ruth is enjoyable simply as a story, it proclaims as well the marvelous universality of the God who "shows no partiality, but in every nation anyone who fears him . . . is acceptable to him" (Acts 10:34-35).

The Story: The Foreigner

(This section is based on the Bible account, scholarly sources, and personal reflection. Let your imagination help you re-create Ruth and Naomi and the story of their lives.)

Ruth was a foreigner to Israel. As a Moabite she was one of those excluded from the congregation of Israel. "No Ammonite or Moabite shall enter the assembly of the Lord; even to the tenth generation none belonging to them shall enter the assembly of the Lord for ever . . ." (Deut. 23:3). Her foreignness seems unduly emphasized in the story: it is mentioned even when it is not necessary to the plot (Ruth 2:2,21).

Yet this "foreigner" is accepted and affirmed by the people of Bethlehem, marries one of their leading citizens, and becomes an ancestor of Israel's greatest king. Who was this remarkable woman?

Unlike many other significant women in the Old Testament, Ruth is never described as beautiful or fair of form and face. She is not famous for her physical appearance. Her beauty lies in strength of character and in a presence that immediately attracts others to her.

Certainly Naomi is a remarkable woman. Even though she informed her old friends in Bethlehem that they must now call her

Mara (1:20) because life has become "bitter" to her, she did not give any evidence of withdrawing from life or of giving up the struggle to survive.

Orpah, the wife of Naomi's son Chilion, showed love and concern for her mother-in-law and was willing to go with her to Bethlehem to live the life of a foreigner there. This decision could not have been made lightly since, in the ancient world, to live as a resident alien meant forfeiting all legal rights. Naomi knew that she could not promise her daughters-in-law any good future in Bethlehem. Although desperation and famine had driven her and her husband to live as aliens in Moab, she was not willing to impose the hardship of that kind of life on the two young women. She knew the hardships to which alien status could expose one and her genuine concern for the young widows motivated her to insist that they go back to their own people and find new husbands who could give them a home and family.

Orpah finally agreed, but Naomi had not reckoned with Ruth's commitment to her that went beyond their legal relationship and found its strength in two other factors. One was the force of a love that transcended age and race and the other was the power of her conversion to the God of Israel.

Perhaps Naomi had unwittingly sharpened Ruth's determination with the statement she made after Orpah left, "See, your sister-in-law has gone back to her people and to her gods; return after your sister-in-law" (1:15).

Ruth could not go back to Chemosh the god of the Moabites (Num. 21:29; Jer. 48:46). She had come to know another God, one who did not demand human sacrifice and who did not condone licentiousness. Their common faith made Ruth more kin to Naomi than to her own father and mother. In her memorable answer to Naomi, she stated her commitment to the God of Israel with the words, "your God [will be] my God" (1:16). She did not use the usual name which foreigners give to God, "Elohim," but used "Yahweh." The writer of the book shows in this way that this particular foreigner was a follower of the true God (*The Interpreter's Bible*, vol. 2, p. 837).

In Bethlehem, Ruth looked for work that would provide some income for them. By chance (or was it chance?) she went to glean grain in the fields of a landowner named Boaz. Gleaners could pick up what was left in the field by the reapers or what was left on vines or fruit trees after the pickers had taken all the ripe fruit. In this way, the poor, the orphan, the widow, and the resident alien—the foreigners in the land—could work and provide for their own needs (Deut. 24:19-22).

What was it about Ruth that caught the eye of Boaz? Was it some dignity of bearing? Or was it the opposite, some delicate physical fragility that was propelled by inner strength to work beyond its own ability? Whatever sparked his early interest in the young Moabite woman, Boaz was so charmed that he moved immediately to make sure that she stayed in *his* fields.

"Drop some extra grain for her," he told the reapers, "and see that none of you molests her in any way."

Boaz knew what dangers life posed for young women who had no protective male to look after them. And she was a foreigner besides. He invited her to eat lunch with him, giving her so much food that she took the leftovers home to Naomi!

Naomi recognized the owner of the field as a relative, one of her nearest of kin, and saw in this fact the providential hand of God. While Ruth worked on the harvest, Naomi worked on a plan.

In Israel, a patriarchal society, only the sons of a man could inherit the property. If a man died without sons, then the nearest of kin could buy the land in order that it might be kept in the family. An even greater responsibility of the nearest of kin was to take the wife of the dead man as his own wife in order that she might bear a son who would then be counted as the son of the dead man and be able to carry on the inheritance and the family name (Deut. 25:5-6). Failure to perform this responsibility was considered a grave dereliction of duty.

Naomi's plan was simply to find a way to get Boaz to perform the duty of a kinsman to Ruth. With the keen sense of a matchmaker motivated by the need to protect her husband's inheritance and lineage, she instructed Ruth in the "levirate" process. Ruth was to wait on the last day of the harvest and after the men had celebrated their work with much food and drink and gone off to sleep, she was to lie at the feet of Boaz until he woke and found her.

Startled and sleepy, he asked, "Who are you?"

The reader of this love story knows by this time that Boaz wants to marry her. He has heard good things about her kindness to her mother-in-law and now he sees that she wants to fulfill her obligation to her dead father-in-law and husband by bearing a child in their memory. And, above all, she wants to bear that child with him, an older man.

There is an obstacle to their marriage, however. It happens that there is a closer relative to Elimelech who must have the right of first choice. The (unnamed) kinsman wanted to buy the property until he learned (from Boaz, of course) that marriage to Ruth, as part of the property, was part of the deal.

Although no fairy tale, the story has a fairy tale ending. The foreigner is acclaimed by the townspeople as a proper wife for Boaz and is given their blessing. Ruth bears a son, Obed, who is given to Naomi to care for. Virtue and love are rewarded, and Ruth earns a place as an ancestor of King David. More important, she is listed as one of the ancestors of Jesus by Matthew (Matt. 1:5), one of five women named in his genealogy.

Patriarchy makes harsh demands on women. Ruth does her duty toward her husband's family, but we are not told whether her own parents were taken care of or whether their inheritance was secure. Poverty was the lot of both Ruth and Naomi without a man in the family. Perhaps this common lot of women is one bond that makes friendship so precious to them.

The Summary: Women as Friends

"But Ruth said, 'Do not press me to leave you and to turn back from your company, for

'wherever you go, I will go,
wherever you live, I will live.
Your people shall be my people,
and your God, my God.
Wherever you die, I will die
and there I will be buried.
May Yahweh do this thing to me

and more also,
if even death should come between us' "
(Ruth 1:16-17 JB).

Perhaps no more beautiful statement of friendship has ever been made. Even though these words have sometimes been spoken by brides to their husbands in the wedding service, it's well for us all to remember that they were originally spoken by a daughter-in-law to her mother-in-law.

Although the book of Ruth has other themes—the universality of God, the love of man and woman, the survival of family life, and the ancestry of King David—its underlying (and rare) theme is the love of two women for one another. Usually the Bible describes close relationships between a man and a woman or between two men, like David and Jonathan. But between Ruth and Naomi there was a bond of friendship and love which was both dignified and intimate. When some authors write about Bible women they tend to overlook this outstanding fact. One such author subtitles his chapter on Ruth, "The Woman Who Won a Husband," which may be the least significant theme in the book. Although a charming love story, that is hardly the reason the book was included in the Old Testament canon. Even in his footnotes to the Harper Study Bible, the commentator quickly diverts the words of Ruth into the bridal pledge.

Love that is universal and undying, a love that is consistent with the description in 1 Corinthians 13 and that exemplifies the kind of friendship Jesus gave as his gift in John 15:15—this is the great underlying theme of Ruth.

Friendship between women is a unique experience. Many men do not know friendship in quite the same way. In his book *The Friendship Factor,* Dr. McGinnis asks, "Why are such friendships so rare among men?" He answers, "Conditioning, of course. In our society, except to shake hands, men are not even allowed to touch each other." He further elaborates that, since so few males have been allowed the luxury of openness and vulnerability in a relationship, they are not aware of the gaping void in their emotional lives. In short, they don't know what they're missing.

A sharing kind of friendship seems to be what Jesus is talking about in John 15:15 when he says, "No longer do I call you servants, for the servant does not know what his master is doing; but I have called you friends, for all that I have heard from my Father I have made known to you." Friends share. Ruth and Naomi experienced that kind of sharing friendship.

Articles are sometimes written about how much women hate to work with, or for, other women. Some probably do have such feelings, but for every one of those women there are hundreds who work together as volunteers, as churchwomen, as neighbors, as disaster relief workers, and in a multitude of networks and support groups to make this world a better place to live. And they work as friends, not as competitors.

Was this what charmed Boaz? Did he see a quality of friendship in Ruth that made him long for that kind of relationship with another human being? As they ate lunch together and met during the harvest, was their conversation a continual sharing of self—their fears, their dreams, their histories? When love grows out of the soil of friendship, marriage becomes the best of relationships.

But for Ruth and Naomi their friendship was enough. As the women of Bethlehem laid the baby Obed in the arms of Naomi, they knew what this friendship had meant to her, and they said, "for your daughter-in-law who loves you, *who is more to you than seven sons,* has borne him" (4:15).

Questions for Reflection

1. Read Ruth 1:12-15. What do you think about Naomi's insistence that her daughters-in-law return to their families when she knew that she was sending them back to their Moabite religion?

2. What do you think of the Israelite system of permitting the poor, widows, orphans, and foreigners to glean in the fields? How does it compare with other "welfare" systems?

3. Describe the man Boaz from his actions toward Ruth as they are outlined in 2:8-16.

4. In the story told in 3:1-14, what is suggested about Naomi's motives in advising Ruth to visit Boaz? How would our society today view the "levirate" (Deut. 25:5-6) custom?

5. Ruth 4:5: What do the words "buying Ruth" say to you about women's lives at that time? What feelings does that phrase arouse in you?

6. Consider the implications of the statement in 4:17. Why was Obed called Naomi's son even though Ruth bore him?

7

1 Samuel 1:1—2:26

HANNAH

The Setting: Shiloh, a Place of Contrast

By the time Hannah lived, about 200 years had passed since the Lord led the Israelites out of bondage in Egypt. The years of wandering in the wilderness were over, and the time of war and slaughter and strife in Canaan had dissipated into tribal squabbles with every man doing "what was right in his own eyes" (Judg. 21:25). Shiloh, a city about 10 miles northeast of Bethel (now called Seilun), is the setting for the last scene in Judges and for the first scene in the books of Samuel.

Shiloh was a place of contrasts. The Ark of the Covenant and the tabernacle which symbolized the presence of God among the people of Israel had rested there. The village was chosen by Joshua for rather vague reasons to become an important Israelite center. It had no significant history linking it to the patriarchs of pre-Egyptian days, but it was comparatively remote from Canaanite occupation at the time Joshua led the Israelite invaders into that land.

During the time of the judges it was a shrine to which regular pilgrimages were made. Judges 21:19 records: "Behold, there is the yearly feast of the Lord at Shiloh, which is north of Bethel, on the east of the highway that goes up from Bethel to Shechem, and south of Lebonah." Evidently some of the Canaanite fertility rites had become part of the worship observances at Shiloh. The kidnap and rape of the daughters of Shiloh who came out to dance during the feast suggests this. Furthermore, Hophni and Phinehas, the sons of Eli who served at Shiloh as priests with their father, "lay with the women who served at the entrance to the tent of meeting" (1 Sam. 2:22), again suggesting the influence of the Canaanite fertility cult at Shiloh. The women may have been serving as temple prostitutes, a practice that crept into the worship of Israel from its Canaanite neighbors.

Three centuries later Amos would denounce this abomination in no uncertain terms, "a man and his father go into the same maiden, so that my holy name is profaned; they lay themselves down beside every altar upon garments taken in pledge; and in the house of their God they drink the wine of those who have been fined" (Amos 2:7b-8).

If worship had degenerated to this point while Eli and his sons were the keepers of the sacred ark, then it is obvious the times were deeply troubled. Chapters 4-7 of 1 Samuel tell us that God could not long tolerate this situation. During a battle with the Philistines, the elders of Israel suggested that the Ark be brought out to the battlefield, as had sometimes been done before to turn the tides of war in their favor (4:3). When the Ark of the Covenant came into the camp and the Philistines were dismayed, the hopes of the army of Israel were raised. But God did not favor a disobedient people, and the battle went against the Israelites. The Philistines slaughtered 30,000, including Eli's sons, and captured the Ark of the Covenant.

Later Jeremiah the prophet reminded the worshipers in the temple at Jerusalem of what had happened at Shiloh: "Go now to my place that was in Shiloh, where I [the Lord] made my name dwell at first, and see what I did to it for the wickedness of my people Israel" (Jer. 7:12).

The loose confederation of tribes could not withstand the constant assaults by the Canaanite tribes, the Philistines, and the pagan religions of the area. Neither could the priests be trusted to hold the people together.

A stronger form of government was needed in this struggle between the faith of the people of God and the culture that was threatening to engulf them. A foreshadowing of what was ahead came in the time of the judge, Gideon. His skills in leadership led the men of Israel to offer him the crown of a king.

"Rule over us," they begged, "you and your son and your grandson also; for you have delivered us out of the hand of Midian" (Judg. 8:22). They saw the need for some form of government that did not depend merely on charismatic leaders.

But at that time Gideon was committed to God's rule over Israel (a "theocracy") and refused, saying, "I will not rule over you, and my son will not rule over you; the Lord will rule over you" (Judg. 8:23).

But when Shiloh fell and the Ark was in the hands of the Philistines, Israel was in a desperate situation. The sanctuary was gone, the priests were dead (Eli fell over dead when he heard of his sons' deaths), and the glory seemed to have departed from Israel (1 Sam. 4:17-18).

But, as we learned in the session on Deborah, the darkest hours in Israel's political history were always the occasion for the people to search their hearts, to repent, and to renew their commitment to the God of the covenant.

Even before this dismal situation reached its climax in Israel, God was preparing for the birth of a leader who would mark the beginning of a new period in Israel's life. Under a new prophetic style of leadership the nation was to move from a tribal confederacy to a monarchy.

The Story: The Mother

(This section is based on the Bible account, scholarly sources, and personal reflection. Let your imagination help you re-create Hannah's experience.)

A woman who prayed was to be the instrument through whom God would save Israel from political and religious disintegration. Her name was Hannah, and she was the childless wife of a man named Elkanah, a member of the tribe of Ephraim who lived in Ramah, 12 miles northwest of Bethel and 12 miles west of Shiloh.

As far as we know Elkanah was an undistinguished man, the descendant of undistinguished men—Zuph, Tohu, Elihu, and Jeroham.

He had two wives, Hannah and Peninnah. The practice of having two wives seems to have been common in Israel, since there was a law regulating how the inheritance was to be divided among sons of the two wives. Apparently, this practice usually led to the preference of one wife over the other, putting in jeopardy the inheritance rights of the firstborn son of the disliked wife. Deuteronomy 21:15-17, however, forbids favoritism.

While well-known Bible characters like Jacob, Gideon, David, and Solomon had many wives, such a practice does not seem to have been as common in Israel as having two wives. In a fascinating little book about the practice of polygamy in Africa today, *My Wife Made Me a Polygamist*, the late Walter Trobisch talks about the challenge that the biblical concept of monogamy (one wife, one husband, Gen. 2:24; Matt. 19:6) presents to both the African church and the western church. Although in Africa a man may have many wives at one time, he points out that in the west we are practicing "successive" polygamy through easy divorce and remarriage.

In the Bible, says Trobisch, "there are different motives leading to polygamy. For Abraham and Elkanah (1 Sam. 2) it was barrenness; for Lamech (Gen. 4:23) it was pride; for Gideon (Judg. 8:30) it was prestige; for Boaz, who married Ruth, the widow of one of his cousins (Ruth 4), it was the levirate marriage; for David and Solomon it was power and sexual lust."

How does a woman feel when she shares her husband with another woman? Apparently, for Hannah it was not Peninnah she objected to; rather, her unhappiness was caused by the fact that the other wife had children but she did not. Do you remember what was said about childlessness in our story about Sarah? The Israelite male had a terror of childlessness since only through the children could he be assured of having his name kept alive among his people. The chief responsibility of a wife in those days was to bear children (sons). If she failed in this respect, she was supposed to share her husband's affections with someone who could make up for her inadequacy (Gen. 16:1-3).

Hannah could not accept her childlessness, and Peninnah, no doubt out of jealousy because Hannah had a greater share of Elkanah's love, never let her forget her failure. Hannah grieved and wept and would not eat. Depression consumed her.

Let's turn from Hannah to Elkanah for a moment. Just as Ruth in our last session defined friendship between women in a way it had never been defined before, so Elkanah described marriage with a spiritual insight that is out of keeping with cultural norms. He saw the relationship of husband and wife as having value in itself entirely apart from the production of children. His words to the distraught Hannah reveal that the union of marriage is a true becoming of "one flesh" (Gen. 2:24) even before the union is demonstrated in the one flesh of a child belonging to both of them.

"Hannah," he said, "why do you weep? And why do you not eat? And why is your heart sad? Am I not more to you than 10 sons?" (1 Sam. 1:8).

Elkanah saw something that Hannah, in her anguished failure to live up to her culture's norms for wives, was incapable of seeing. He saw that, while children are an additional blessing in a marriage, marriage has meaning even without children. The deepest meaning of marriage lies in the freely given love between a wife and a husband. Elkanah longed for that kind of love from Hannah.

But Hannah, needing the affirmation of the society in which she lived, prayed for a child. "Make me a mother," she cried. "If you do, I'll dedicate the baby (God, make it a boy!) to you."

A selfish, bargaining prayer if there ever was one, isn't it? After all, she didn't need the baby for her husband; he already had children.

But the Lord heard her prayer. And the next time Elkanah and Hannah made love, "the Lord remembered her" (1:19), the Bible's way of saying that she became pregnant at that time.

Hannah lost no time in fulfilling her promise to the Lord. She nursed the baby until he was two or three years old, weaned him, and brought him back to the priest at Shiloh.

"Remember me?" she asked Eli. "I'm the woman you thought was drunk when I was praying. Here's the answer to my prayer, my son Samuel. I am lending him to the Lord. Take him."

How could Hannah leave a toddler with men like Eli and his sons (2:12)? How could she and Elkanah just turn around and go back home to Ramah? As simple as her prayer was, so simple seems Hannah's trust in her Lord. Giving up her son did not mean giving up her primary responsibility for him. Although she left him in the temple, she never ceased caring for him. Every year she made a little robe for him and brought it to the temple in Shiloh. We can be quite sure that every stitch was a prayer and every visit a joyful reunion. Samuel was not abandoned. He knew he was loved by his parents, his brothers and sisters, and by God.

When we consider what God accomplished through the man Samuel (3:19—4:1), we see how God uses pain and grief to motivate us to fervent prayer so that his purposes may be accomplished. Had Hannah been willing to accept her husband's loving devotion as a substitute for her heart's desire to have a baby, Israel may have been denied prophetic leadership at a crucial time in its history. When the psalmist says that the Lord "will give you the desires of your heart," does it not also mean that God puts those desires into one's heart? Hannah acted in response to the holy discontent beyond all rational understanding that the Spirit often stirs up in our hearts.

The Summary: Women as Pray-ers

Have you ever prayed so deeply that you lost awareness of the external world? Eli, the priest, was sitting by the doorpost of the temple when he noticed a woman standing in prayer, her lips moving but no sound coming out. He immediately assumed that she had been celebrating a little too much at the annual "Yahweh's feast" (Judg. 21:19-21) and was under the influence of alcohol. It was apparently the custom at that time to pray out loud in the temple or Eli would not have thought it strange that Hannah was praying silently. Her incoherence signified drunkenness to him.

Two facts from Hannah's method of prayer seem appropriate for us to consider here. First of all, why is it so difficult for us to pray out loud today? Why do the most vocal among us often become so tongue-tied in prayer? Perhaps part of our difficulty comes from having had our grammar and words corrected too much when we were learning to speak. Words get in our way and we become self-conscious. Public prayer, we seem to feel, is appropriate for pastors, pastors' spouses, Bible study leaders, and other "professional pray-ers."

Hannah had no training in prayer, and her theological understandings of the nature of prayer can be questioned by theologians. She was bitter. She bargained with God (1 Sam. 1:10-11). *But Hannah prayed!* Publicly. And even though her voice was soft and perhaps hoarse with the intensity of emotion, she prayed. God does not regard professionalism in prayer as important. It's the heart that matters and the fact that one prays at all.

Second, how difficult it is for us to get lost in prayer, so that external realities fade away and we are only aware of the presence of our Lord. Perhaps in our hurried world that requires too much time. How long does it take for you to let go of that list of responsibilities you carry around in your head and to become aware only of the voice of the Lord? Ten minutes? An hour? When Hannah stood in the temple and prayed, it was obviously not her first prayer. Centering so completely on the presence of God that one becomes oblivious to all external distractions requires practice. Knowing all about prayer comes with *doing* prayer.

Have you noticed how many lessons are taught and sermons preached on Hannah's prayer before Samuel was born and how little is said about her prayer in the temple after his birth? Thanksgiving and praise arc also prayer and are a part of our conversations with God. Some biblical scholars wonder if the words of the prayer in Chapter 2 were actually composed by Hannah or if they represent a psalm written at another time. Certainly its tone differs greatly from her words and manner before Samuel's birth, but at the same time we recognize that the difference can be attributed to the difference between words spoken in grief and those spoken in joy and celebration.

"God cares for me! God cares for all people! Nothing happens that God does not know about since the whole world rests on foundations created by God the Almighty!" When we have seen God's action on our behalf, our prayers ring with certainty and shouts of joy which are incompatible with grief and despair.

Praise intensifies prayer by focusing our attention on the actions of God rather than on our own needs and concerns. Evelyn Underhill, the famed mystic, learned to contemplate all of the objects of creation until she could praise the creator in and through the object. Anything will do, she says. Then, "pour yourself out towards it, do not draw its image towards you" (Evelyn Underhill, *Practical Mysticism*, p. 93). In doing so you will rediscover praise through the marvelous miracles that occur every day in the hands of the Creator: a chick pecking its way out of the eggshell, a butterfly being born from a cocoon, the rising and setting of the sun, the budding of a rose, the fingernails of a baby.

Through Jesus the Redeemer we can draw near to God the Creator with the understanding that majesty and might are also redeeming mercy. The power of God responds to the mercy of God and, in Hannah's situation, God said yes to her need for a baby. Little wonder that her song of praise became the model for Mary's Magnificat (Luke 1:46-55). Both were born out of the overwhelming acknowledgment that the God of all creation and of all creatures listens to and answers the prayers of people of faith everywhere and in all times.

Questions for Reflection

1. What insight into the nature of marriage relationships does the storyteller reveal in 1 Sam. 1:8? How does this perception contradict the cultural view that a woman's value was measured by her ability to have children?

2. Hannah prays very specifically for a son in 1:11. How do you feel about praying that specifically? When might a request turn into dictating to God?

3. Read 1:10-20. Make a list of some principles of prayer found in this account. Hannah struck a bargain with God. How do you feel about this kind of prayer?

4. Hannah believed that God had given Samuel to her, so she kept her promise and gave him back to God (v. 28). In what ways do parents "give their children back to God?"

5. Read Hannah's song of praise in 2:1-10. How is God described in this poetry? Is Hannah's understanding of the nature of God similar to yours? How can this text be a sign of hope for poor people?

8

2 Samuel 11:1—12:24

BATHSHEBA

The Setting: Israel Demands a King

Samuel, the son for whom Hannah prayed, became the last judge of Israel. As a great prophet and spiritual leader, his influence on the history of Israel can be compared with that of Moses. His career as a judge-prophet-priest began in Shiloh at the time of the Philistine victory over Israel and their capture of the Ark of the Covenant, symbol of God's presence among the people of Israel. The old priest Eli and his sons were dead, and young Samuel was serving in the temple.

When he was old, Samuel hoped his sons would carry on the judgeship, but they were not men like their father. So the elders of Israel came to Samuel at Ramah (1 Sam. 8:4).

"You are old," they said, "and your sons do not walk in your ways; now appoint for us a king to govern us like all the nations" (8:5).

Samuel objected to this request for a king and refused it (1 Sam. 8:6-22). The Lord finally told him to give the people their way even though the request was interpreted to be a rejection of God (8:7-9).

So Israel was given a king named Saul as a rather grudging concession, since becoming "like all the nations" meant that Israel's identity as "the people of God" was being compromised. God alone was to be ruler. As the year passed, the monarchy demanded by the people was plagued by internal strife, murders, jealousy, ambition, and lust.

Saul, the first king, was replaced by David in the 11th century
B.C. Under his leadership the agonizing conquest of Canaan finally
came to an end. David also took the Jebusite fortress of Jerusalem
and made it his capital. As neutral territory on the boundary between
northern and southern Israel, it gave David a vantage point from
which to create a united kingdom.

By the age of 37, David had proved himself a shrewd political
leader and a brilliant military commander, ruling over an empire
that stretched from Lebanon in the north to the borders of Egypt
in the south and from the Mediterranean Sea to the Arabian desert.
David was the beloved of the Lord as the biblical author writes,
"And David became greater and greater, for the Lord, the God of
hosts, was with him" (2 Sam. 5:10).

One of his greatest accomplishments was to bring the Ark of the
Covenant out of the oblivion in which it had languished ever since
the Philistines had decided to get it out of their land (1 Sam. 5–6).
"So David went and brought up the ark of God from the house of
Obed-edom to the city of David with rejoicing; . . . And David
danced before the Lord with all his might . . . " (2 Sam. 6:12-14).

David had an energetic spirit and his exuberance was contagious.
One man, however, was not subject to David's magnetism. A prophet
named Nathan became the voice of God announcing limits on David's
ambitions and his self-indulgent abuse of power.

Nathan gave David a gentle rebuke from the Lord when he pro-
posed to put the Ark of the Covenant in a house of cedar instead of
leaving it in the tent where it had been placed after its arrival in
Zion. Nathan reminded him that God preferred the tent (2 Sam.
7:4-7). When David surrendered to God's will he was given the
promise, "your throne shall be established for ever" (7:16).

But Nathan's most stinging message from the Lord was to come
when David's power was at its peak and when he was most certain
that he was the favored son of the Lord.

Like King Saul before him, David had one particularly serious
flaw in his character. Saul's downfall was an obsessive jealousy that
became a psychosis. When Samuel rebuked Saul for his disobedience
to God with these words, "The Lord has torn the kingdom of Israel
from you this day, and has given it to a neighbor of yours [David],

who is better than you" (1 Sam. 15:28), Saul's jealousy literally drove him crazy. He tried to kill David; he alienated his own son; he killed 85 priests. And the Lord gave his throne to David.

But David, too, had a weakness in his character. He felt that he had the right to take any woman he wanted for his own pleasure or for power.

David was charming. As a musician, he had talent enough to charm away the madness in King Saul (1 Sam. 16:23). As a friend, he was able to form close and loyal relationships (1 Sam. 20:17). As a gifted and charismatic leader, he was able to command the devotion of multitudes (2 Sam. 6:14-15).

Born with such gifts and being the youngest of the eight sons of Jesse (1 Sam. 17:12-14), David had every reason to be "spoiled," with his every childhood whim immediately gratified. So when David grew up and saw a woman he wanted, he took her. He had many wives, among them Michal, daughter of King Saul (1 Sam. 18:27), whose "bride-price" was the foreskins of 200 slain Philistines; Abigail, the wife of his dead enemy, Nabal (1 Sam. 25:42); Ahinoam of Jezreel (1 Sam. 25:43); Maacah; Haggith; Abital; Eglah; and Bathsheba; and many concubines (1 Chron. 3:1-9).

Our story has to do with the unbelievably sordid events leading to David's marriage with Bathsheba and with the consequences following those actions.

The Story: The Bathing Beauty

(This section is based on the Bible account, scholarly sources, and personal reflection. Let your imagination help you re-create Bathsheba's experience.)

The scenario is a familiar one. A beautiful young woman was bathing and a middle-aged man, walking on his rooftop, saw her. The man was a powerful ruler over many nations, with many children by several wives. Applauded by the people, he was respected by his courtiers and military generals. He had everything he needed or wanted—except this young woman.

Stories of lust, seduction, rape, and murder make good scripts for Hollywood. They are so commonplace as to be boring. But outside the movie theaters and away from the television screens, they chronicle human suffering, pain, and degradation.

A young woman was taken and raped. No matter how delicately biblical language puts it, and no matter what the status of women was in that day, that is really what the story of Bathsheba is all about. The young wife of a devoted soldier was taken out of her home by the commander-in-chief of her husband's army, the king of her country, and forced to have intercourse with him.

A familiar reaction to this story is to excuse David, the greatest of Israel's kings, and to blame the beautiful young woman. And some writers have done this. Harold Ockenga in his book *Women Who Made Bible History* does so. Why was she bathing where she could be seen? Why was she so immodest? Her pain is ignored.

Have you found yourself blaming the woman who is raped? "It's because women dress the way they do," a judge says. Or, "she should have fought him off," we hear.

(Just so there will be no misunderstanding about the "uncleanness" referred to in 2 Sam. 11:4, this is the Bible's way of saying that she had just finished menstruating [Lev. 15:19-24], a period during which women were considered ritually "unclean." This may have been the reason she was bathing herself so thoroughly.)

Statements which make women suspects in cases of rape have kept women the silent victims. For many women who, like Bathsheba, have been violated sexually, the situation is no-win. Could Bathsheba have said no to David? Given the fact that a girl was brought up to believe that she was subject to the authority of men all of her life, first to her father and then to her husband and sons, it was unlikely that she could easily have said no to the most powerful authority figure in her world. Besides, she may have feared what might happen to her husband if she refused his military commander. Would he be treated badly, given tougher duty, perhaps refused promotions and benefits? Many women tell of being forced to exchange sexual favors for good grades, jobs, promotions, or friendship.

No matter which way she turned, there was no way out for Bathsheba. The messengers of David "took her" (2 Sam. 11:4). She was given no choice when the summons came to go to the king. The discovery of her pregnancy also meant death for her. Hebrew law put it this way: "If a man commits adultery with the wife of his neighbor, both the adulterer and the adulteress shall be put to death" (Lev. 20:10).

Now we begin to understand David's desire to bring Uriah back home and arrange for him to sleep with his wife! David's life was also in jeopardy. But Uriah was too dedicated a soldier to enjoy the comforts of home while his companions were still on the battlefield. David himself recognized abstinence from sexual relations as a requirement for those men who were on a military expedition (1 Sam. 21:4-5).

None of David's schemes worked. He tried in vain to get Uriah drunk enough to want to sleep in his own house, but instead Uriah went out to sleep with David's servants. Thus, sin leads to its inevitable end. David ordered his general Joab to put Uriah, man of integrity and valor, in the middle of the fiercest battle and to leave him there, unprotected, to die.

When Bathsheba heard that her husband had died in battle, did she have any idea of the things that had been happening at the palace? Did anyone tell her that Uriah had been in the city but had not come home to her? Was she hiding out in fear, refusing to open the door to anyone lest someone suspect her condition or ask embarrassing questions? Imagine the loneliness and isolated suffering that a girl of 15 or 16, her probable age, must have felt.

We will never know the answer to all of these questions, of course, but the Bible does tell us that when she got the news of Uriah's death (did a message come from the king himself?), she "made lamentation for her husband" (2 Sam. 11:26). If the description of the poor man's relationship to his ewe lamb (12:3) is an indication of the relationship between Uriah and Bathsheba—"it used to eat of his morsel, and drink from his cup, and lie in his bosom, and it was like a daughter to him"—then we can understand Bathsheba's mourning. That kind of tender love was not what David had shown her.

To David's credit, he did marry Bathsheba. He could have taken her as another concubine, but it's possible that his conscience was a little troubled even though his comment to Joab on hearing of Uriah's death reveals callousness, "Do not let this matter trouble you, for the sword devours now one and now another" (2 Sam. 11:25).

In his condemnation of David's actions against Uriah and Bathsheba, Nathan pictured Bathsheba as the innocent victim. We need to remember this lest we be tempted to join those who would like to make the victim responsible for her victimization. She suffered jointly with David in the death of their baby boy (2 Sam. 12:24) but lived to rejoice when her son Solomon was given the throne of Israel over all of David's other legitimate sons (1 Kings 1:28-31).

Reading about David's behavior toward Bathsheba brings heartache to those of us who love him for his exuberance, his love of the Lord and the people of Israel, his reverence for the Ark, and for his love of music and poetry. Nevertheless, the deterioration of David's children, their troubles, and their sins reminds us that "all have sinned and fall short of the glory of God," and that God visits the sins of the fathers on their children (Exod. 20:5).

For all the Bathshebas of this world, victims of lust and brutality, condemned by their societies to stoning or drowning or burning because they were victims of rape and adultery, Jesus Christ brought the first word of hope and release when he wrote in the sand and invited anyone "who is without sin among you" to cast the first stone of condemnation (John 8:7).

The Summary: Women as Survivors

Many women have proven to be good survivors.

While we do not hear much about Bathsheba in her early days as the wife of David, she apparently did not sit around bemoaning her fate as a member of David's ample harem. Physical beauty was not her only endowment; she also possessed intelligence and wisdom. Her influence in the court of David grew. Much younger than David, she was strong and vigorous when he was an old man.

While the old king was sick and dying, the struggle for the throne began. Adonijah, son of David's wife Haggith, began to gather political supporters who recognized him as the eldest living son and therefore the logical successor (1 Kings 1:5-7).

Now David had secretly promised Bathsheba that her son Solomon would be king after him. Bathsheba remembered, as did Nathan, the old prophet. Knowing Bathsheba's influence over the king, Nathan suggested that she go into the king's bedroom and remind him of his promise before he died. Nathan's respect for Bathsheba apparently had grown with the years. Her request to the dying king was a remarkable speech (1 Kings 1:16-21) that accomplished its purpose. Solomon became a king.

What a different person this Bathsheba was from the young, passive, frightened girl forced to have sex with David. She had grown to a position of influence in a situation that she did not seek but that she accepted and used as an opportunity to grow. Adonijah, the crown prince whose attempt to seize power failed, even went to Bathsheba to ask for a favor. Would she go to her son on Adonijah's behalf and ask for the young woman who had served his father David during his dying days? (1 Kings 2:13-18). Things did not work out as requested, but the plea was a testimony to Bathsheba's influence at court.

How many women throughout history have suffered personal violence, the hardships of war? How many have become refugees and wanderers, have been hungry and destitute? Yet they go on living, surviving as best they can, often with many children for whom to provide. In the process many grow strong and develop the ability to get what they need to live and to grow.

David's second wife, Abigail, for example, made herself known to David as a woman of charm and intelligence when she intervened on her churlish husband's behalf during a quarrel with David. She did not sit around bemoaning her first husband's stupidity but did what she could to prevent his ill nature from bringing calamity on the entire household, including herself (1 Sam. 25). After her husband's death David asked her to be his wife, and she lost no time in joining him.

If to survive means to live or continue beyond the death of another, that's exactly what women have had to learn to do. Because men have a shorter life expectancy, women often outlive men. Unless we learn to take care of ourselves, we are doomed.

Today women are working with each other to protect themselves against sexual abuse and rape and are concerned with the victimization of other women. Do you remember the war in Bangladesh in

1971 and the rape of about 300,000 Bengali women by Pakistani soldiers? Thousands of them became pregnant and, by tradition, no Moslem husband would take back a wife who had been touched by another man. When this story broke in U.S. papers, organized protest came from many sources. While wartime rape has been commonplace in the history of all peoples, this may have been the first time that worldwide indignation was aroused.

The Bangladesh Central Organization for Women's Rehabilitation was created by Bengali women themselves. Most of the women treated were found to have venereal disease, wanted abortions rather than to bear the babies of rape, had psychological and emotional problems, had tried self-abortion with whatever means were at hand, and were all rejected by their families or husbands. But the women gave each other tenderness, shelter, and the skills necessary to support themselves.

The tragedy for women is that Bangladesh is not a unique situation, except in the international attention it received. Under repressive regimes in Latin America women are singled out for torture, usually involving rape or mutilation, a reality that has become an issue for women's organizations in Latin America. In all of our communities the plight of women of all ages from two years to ninety years of age who are attacked by men needs the attention of all women and men. The violently sexual nature of movies and television programs and the availability of sadomasochistic erotic literature makes concerted action necessary.

At the very least, let us care about each other and be quick to comfort and slow to condemn when women are exploited. It is up to each one of us to help each other live in joy and freedom. Jesus did much to change the attitudes toward women by affirming the value of all persons.

As God pronounced his judgment on the sin of David, so we are called to live in purity and respect with each other. Let there be no more Bathshebas if we can help it.

Questions for Reflection

1. Read 2 Samuel 11. In verses 1-2, what connection do you see between the moral character of what was happening in the kingdom and David's personal behavior?

2. What was David trying to accomplish (2 Sam. 11:6-15) in the light of who he was, his position in life, and his call to serve the Lord? Give present day examples of an official trying to cover up wrongdoing.

3. Do you think Uriah ever knew what was happening to his wife or to himself? In what ways might we be unwittingly manipulated by others for their advantage?

4. What seems to be David's understanding of prayer as demonstrated by his behavior in 12:21-23? What examples of God's love and mercy do you see in these chapters?

ESTHER

The Setting: In the Days of Ahasuerus

The story of Esther poses some puzzling questions. Is it an historical novel? Does it take a Persian religious myth about the gods Marduk and Ishtar and use it to disguise a book of encouragement to Jews under persecution? Does it represent actual historical occurrences? Is it fiction, written to demonstrate God's faithfulness to Jews in exile?

The unknown author of the book of Esther possessed inside knowledge of Persian palaces and customs, a fact confirmed by archeologists and historians. At the same time it contains some historical inaccuracies, since Xerxes (485–465 B.C.), the Persian king called Ahasuerus in the book of Esther, did not have a queen named Vashti or Esther. Rather, his queen was a Persian general's daughter named Amestris. Nor is there any historical evidence of any general persecution of the Jewish exiles during Xerxes' reign.

Some have thought Esther was queen to Artaxerxes II (404–358 B.C.) whom history records as having a queen named Stateira, thought by some to be the same as the Hebrew Vashti. In addition, an important discovery in the early 1940s of a cuneiform (early stone writing) text refers to a high official at the court of Susa during the reign of Xerxes named Marduka or Mordecai.

The best interpretation for the book of Esther is that it is based on actual events but was written in the form of a historical novel.

One of the immediate facts to strike the Bible student is the absence of any reference to God or religion in the entire book! It's the only book in the Bible of this nature. In fact, Martin Luther rejected the book, insisting that it had no place in the Bible. In one of his "table talks" he said, "I am so hostile to the book (2 Maccabees) and to Esther that I wish they did not exist at all; for they Judaize too much and have much heathen perverseness."

On the other hand, Jews through the ages have prized this book so highly that some rabbis have believed that, even if all the other prophetic books were forgotten, Esther would always be remembered. Every year it is read at the Feast of Purim, a festival commemorating the deliverance of the Jews. Pürim means "lots" and is derived from the *Pür* cast by Haman to determine the most propitious day for slaughtering all of the Jews in the Persian empire (Esther 3:7). The lots finally fell on the 13th day of the Hebrew month of Adar. Now the Feast of Purim is celebrated annually on the 14th and 15th days of the Hebrew month of Adar, around the first of March.

Since Purim is a time of riotous celebrating with much drinking, eating, and reveling, some have concluded that all references to the name of God were deliberately left out of the book in order that the Lord's name not be read in such a secularized context. Purim is never identified as a "holy day" but is much beloved by Jews as the only feast day that allows for unrestrained merriment to a people who are usually somber and mournful in their religious observances.

Tragically, history is full of massacres of Jews. In our day the Holocaust under Hitler was the worst of them all. "Why," we ask, "why so much hatred toward the Jewish people?"

Haman accused them of being a separate people, keeping to themselves and keeping their own laws and observances no matter what the laws and observances were of all other people in the land. But God called them to be a separate people, and throughout history they have taken their "chosenness" seriously.

The people's love of the story of Esther persuaded the Jews to include it in their Scriptures even though there was some debate about the matter. *The Interpreter's Bible* describes the importance of the book for the Jewish people.

The book of Esther has always been for Jews an allegory depicting the Jewish life and Jewish lot among the nations. It is a book in which not just one period is depicted, but all periods; it is a book that remains forever new because Jewish enemies will not allow it to grow old. It is a book that breathes of love for Jews, of the tie that unites the Jews . . ." (vol. 3, p. 833).

Even in Persia, the most powerful kingdom of its day, God remembered and rescued his people because one Jewish woman was willing to risk her life to accomplish that purpose. What a story! What a woman!

The Story: Queen Esther

(This section is based on the Bible account, scholarly sources, and personal reflection. Let your imagination help you re-create Esther's experience.)

Life in a palace! Like Cinderella of the fairy tale, Hadassah, the beautiful Jewish orphan, became Queen Esther, wife of the most powerful ruler of her day. However, unlike the Prince Charming of the fairy tale, Esther's husband was a tyrant who demanded absolute and immediate obedience from subjects all over his kingdom.

His first wife had been sent into exile for daring to refuse one of his requests. Vashti, queen of Persia before Esther, was quite an extraordinary woman. Even though she had full knowledge of the consequences of disobeying one of her husband's orders, she said no to him.

The request? "Come and show your beauty to all the people of Susa and the visiting dignitaries at the elaborate banquet I'm giving in celebration of my greatness! I want them all to marvel at the beauty of my chief treasure, Queen Vashti!"

Sounds easy, doesn't it? But for Vashti it meant personal degradation to be summoned like a slave to exhibit herself before crowds of drunken revelers. She was a queen and therefore to be treated with respect; not as part of the king's collection of women. So she refused, and for that refusal Vashti deserves our admiration. By placing great value on her person she encourages other women to do the same.

To make an example of her, her crown was taken away, she was banished from the presence of the king to the harem for discarded women, never to marry again or bear children.

When the king sobered up after the banquet and his anger died down, he evidently missed his lovely queen. But Persian kings did not change their minds. A saying has come down from those times to describe rules that are as rigid and unchangeable as "the laws of the Persians and the Medes" (1:13-15,19).

The servants of King Ahasuerus knew what it would take to make their master happy again. "Let beautiful young virgins be sought out for the king," they advised, and a massive beauty contest was launched throughout the kingdom. The participants were not volunteers, however, but were taken forcibly by military officers.

One of the girls brought to the palace was Hadassah, a maiden "beautiful and lovely" and a Jew whose great-grandparents had been among the captives carried away from Jerusalem by Nebuchadnezzar, king of Babylon. Since her parents were dead, she had been adopted by her cousin Mordecai.

Apparently there was some feeling against Jews in those days, and Mordecai told Hadassah to keep her Jewish identity a secret. For 12 months the young girls were bathed, oiled, anointed, perfumed, and given instructions by the eunuch (a castrated man) in charge of the harem. Then each would be sent, one at a time, to the king in the evening and sent back to another harem in the morning to become one of his concubines. Some would never be called again and would remain imprisoned in the second harem forever.

Something about Hadassah pleased the king more than all the others and she was crowned Queen Esther, successor to Vashti, four years after Vashti's courageous act and deposition. Truly Esther's is a "Cinderella story," but one with a much more complicated plot.

The time came when cousin Mordecai incurred the anger and hatred of Haman, Ahasuerus's "prime minister," by refusing to prostrate himself before him. Haman is identified as an Agagite (Esther 3:1), interpreted by the ancient historian Josephus to mean "Amalekite," descendants of Esau and traditional enemies of Israel (Deut. 25:17-19), and this fact may be the reason for Mordecai's refusal to bow before him.

Haman's hatred for Mordecai was projected on all the Jews in all of the provinces ruled by Persia, and he persuaded the king to issue a decree for their annihilation.

Esther had now been queen of Persia for about six years. The time had come for her destiny as queen to be revealed. Her cousin Mordecai sent her a message and reminded her of her true identity. She was a Jew and *all* Jews, men, women, and children, were to be killed on the same day.

"It's up to you," Mordecai's message said. "Who knows whether you have not come to the kingdom for such a time as this?"

But Esther had not been called to the king's bedroom for 30 days. Did she wonder if he were growing tired of her? After all, he had his choice of many beautiful women. She, like Vashti, could be replaced. Beauty fades and love can be fickle, she may have thought. And to go to the king unannounced could mean instant death.

Esther hesitated. Only a fool steps into certain death without thinking. At last a plan worthy of a great diplomat became clear to her. But first she prepared herself by three days of complete fasting. The Greek translation of the Hebrew Bible (Septuagint) adds a more religious note with these words:

"Queen Esther also took refuge with the Lord in the mortal peril which had overtaken her. She took off her sumptuous robes and put on sorrowful mourning. Instead of expensive perfumes she covered her head with ashes and dung. She humbled her body severely, and the former scenes of her happiness and elegance were now littered with tresses torn from her hair" (Esther 4:17 JB).

Then follows a long prayer. The Septuagint further interprets 5:1 with these words.

Radiant as she then appeared, she invoked God who watches over all men and saves them. Then she took two maids with her. With a delicate air she leaned on one, while the other accompanied her carrying her train. She leaned on the maid's arm as though languidly, but in fact because her body was too weak to support her; the other maid followed her mistress, lifting her robes which swept the ground. Rosy with the full flush of her beauty, her face radiated joy and love: but her heart shrank with fear (Esther 5:1a-1b JB).

Even though the Hebrew Bible does not mention God or prayer, one can read much religious content into Esther's fasting, with the knowledge that her decision required great dedication and courage.

With new authority Esther told Mordecai to gather all the Jews in Susa to fast with her. Formerly, Esther's submission and obedience to Mordecai is noted (Esther 2:20). Now, however, we are told that Mordecai "went away and did everything as Esther had ordered him" (4:17). The girl queen had become God's woman, speaking with God's own wisdom and authority. Her purpose and plan were known only to her and her Lord. She went to the king, her life in her hands.

The king's scepter was stretched out to her; she touched it and, with disarming charm, she invited him and Haman to dinner that evening. How wise not to have blurted out her real need!

With even greater restraint, Esther carried off the dinner as though nothing else were on her mind and invited them both to dinner again the next night. Haman was so charmed that he went home and built a gallows 83 feet high on which to hang Mordecai!

The king went to bed but couldn't sleep. So he called for his book of memorable deeds and there read about the time Mordecai saved him from an assassination plot. "How has this man been honored?" he asked.

The next day the king ordered Haman to honor Mordecai. Fear began to form in Haman and we sense the dread that accompanied him to Esther's second banquet. The climax came swiftly as Esther, confident that the right moment to reveal Haman's plot against her and her people had come, pointed an accusing finger at Haman.

Haman died on the gallows he had prepared for Mordecai. Esther was saved and Mordecai took Haman's place as grand vizier to the king. Instead of the wholesale slaughter of Jews on the 13th of Adar, it was the enemies of the Jews who were slaughtered.

And on the 14th and 15th days of Adar the Jews celebrated their escape from destruction with "gladness and feasting and holiday-making" (Esther 9:19), and the first Feast of Purim was held as

Mordecai and Queen Esther "laid down for themselves and for their descendants" (9:31).

The Summary: Women as Risk-Takers

The need for safety and a sense of worth

How can a woman like Esther, whom society and the death of her parents had forced into a dependent condition, ever get to the point where she can make a decision independently?

The potential for acting autonomously is present in every one of us from the time of our birth. Watch children at play. They move freely, exploring, testing, risking. The one requirement for believing that they can do whatever is needed to be done is a healthy sense of their own worth. The adults in their lives need to provide children with safety and security as they venture forth to build positive self-concepts.

Even though Esther's society said women were totally dependent on men, she was given all the ingredients needed to see herself as an acceptable and able person. Mordecai gave her a good loving home, and in addition nature had provided her with great beauty. For most of her life, Esther was content to live the secure role of a beautiful and pampered female. Why struggle to grow up and be an autonomous person if your cocoon is so comfortable? Protection from the hardships of a difficult and demanding world is not easily given up.

Moving out

Esther had moved from Mordecai's house to the palace where she was probably not permitted even to leave her quarters except when called for by the king. In a situation like that only a powerful crisis can force one to independent action. Even so, many women would have simply retreated further into dependency, yielding to their fears, and would have refused to take the risk Esther took.

Struggle often accompanies the decision to move out of safety into the unknown. One feels trapped by life; the walls close in around us. Feelings of loneliness, of being abandoned and forsaken, are common. The future is a frightening void, a great unknown.

Sources of strength

"Unless we can find some stirring of strength in ourselves, or unless God moves in, there's no place to go but to suicide, alcohol, drugs, new dependencies" (Wold, *The Critical Moment*, p. 41). Esther knew where to find strength. In fasting she defied dependency, comfort, and safety; in calling for the support of all of the Susa Jews and her own maidens, she moved from aloneness to community.

Our strength comes from moving inward to our own spiritual resources and from moving outward to the community of believers. Don't be afraid to ask others to support you in your times of tough decision making. Loving sisters and brothers, like the "maids" of Esther, will form a community of strength for you. Esther's maids were probably not Jews, an indication that valuable friends are to be found everywhere.

Benefits and Perils of Risk Taking

Personal growth is the benefit of autonomous action. We become that "self-actualizing" person at the peak of the scale of self-development.

On the other hand, we can be killed, imprisoned, divorced, or misunderstood as a result of risking. That's what risk means—to expose oneself to hazard or danger. The risk is always, "and if I perish, I perish" (4:1b).

But you will never know what the outcome will be unless you dare to risk. One psychologist has written two epitaphs:

She couldn't try
for fear she'd die;
She never tried
and so she died.

She couldn't try
for fear she'd die

But once she tried,
her fears, they died.

Which one would you rather have?

Questions for Reflection

1. Read Esther 1:1-12. If you were Queen Vashti, how would you have responded to the king's command?

2. Read Esther 3:1-6. How is it possible for one human being to plan the destruction of an entire race? Hitler and Stalin were modern day Hamans. Should Mordecai have apologized to Haman in an effort to prevent the slaughter of his people? (Would you?)

3. Have you ever been in a situation as stressful as the one Esther was in? How did you handle it? What did Esther do to combat stress? Read Esther 4:15-16. What support group did Esther have? Consider the importance of support groups for women today.

4. Read Esther 9:1-16. What do you think about the revenge Mordecai and Esther took on the Persian people? Are we to model our behavior after theirs? How does her request in 9:12-14 affect your feelings about her?

10

Luke 1 and 2
(Supplementary texts: Matthew 1 and 2; Luke 8:19-21; John 2:1-11; 19:25-27)

MARY

The Setting: When the Time Had Fully Come

According to the Gospel accounts, Jesus saw women and men as equals in every way. He numbered women among his followers, his images of women were never negative, he went out of his way to give them insights into the nature of his mission, he entrusted them with the proclamation of the gospel, and he used them in his stories and sayings to illustrate theological truths. In the story of the woman and the lost coin (Luke 15:8-10), he even used a woman to describe God seeking lost persons!

Jesus geared his messages to women as well as men, evidently expecting them to be in the crowds who followed him around Palestine. In Luke's account, if Jesus gave an illustration featuring a man, he often gave one featuring a woman.

Look at some of these "paired" parables and illustrations in the gospel of Luke. The healing of a man on the Sabbath (Luke 14:2-6) is placed next to the healing of a woman on the Sabbath (13:10-17). Jesus raised the daughter of a man (8:49-56), and he also raised the son of a woman (7:11-17). The grain of mustard seed that a man took and sowed is like the leaven that a woman took and hid (13:18-21). When Jesus comes again, there will be two men sleeping and two women grinding; one of each pair will be taken and the other left (17:34-35).

When it came to marriage, Jesus questioned the double standard that men practiced in his time (and even in our time), and saw both marriage partners as equally responsible in the relationship. In Mark 10:1-12 Jesus is questioned regarding the legality of divorce. The law allowed divorce only to the man. Jesus' reply to the disciples put both sexes on the same level. Who ever heard of a woman having such rights and responsibilities? Matthew added that the disciples found such newness for wives rather hard to take, saying, "If such is the case of a man with his wife, it is not expedient to marry!" (Matt. 19:10).

According to Jesus, women are not to be regarded as sex objects. He is recorded as saying, "You have heard that it was said, 'You shall not commit adultery.' But I say to you that every one who looks at a woman lustfully has already committed adultery with her in his heart" (Matt. 5:27-28). To Jesus women were created not only for motherhood but also to be his disciples in the entire spectrum of vocations, including theological study (see his response to the woman who blessed Mary's womb and breasts [Luke 11:27-28] and his encouragement to Mary of Bethany [Luke 10:42]).

We do not have space in such a brief study to record all of the wonderfully liberating statements and actions of Jesus, but those actions and words are a basis for change for women.

Jesus was born into this world, according to the Scriptures, "when the time had fully come" (Gal. 4:4), when everything was ready. The *pax romana* kept the nations of that time at a temporary truce; Roman roads set the stage for missionary travel; Greek marketplace speech (*koine*) was common to that world of Roman rule and, as the language of the New Testament, was understood by readers everywhere.

The Old Testament Scriptures heightened the expectancy with descriptions of the one who was to come. Matthew reminded his Jewish audience that this hope of Israel had been fulfilled in Jesus. The place: Bethlehem, in the land of Judah, as prophesied by Micah (Matt. 2:6; Mic. 5:2). His name? Jesus-Emmanuel, as foretold by Isaiah (Matt. 1:23; Isa. 7:14).

And the woman who would bring him into the world? "Behold, a virgin shall conceive and bear a son. . . ." Mary was her name.

The Story: The Lonely Teenager

(This section is based on the Bible account, scholarly sources, personal reflection. Let your imagination help you re-create Mary's experience.)

We know so little about Mary, the mother of Jesus, from the Bible. Each gospel writer has given us a different portrait of her. Each one has emphasized different aspects of her life and ministry. Quite likely Mary was not more than 14 years of age when she was given to Joseph in marriage.

When betrothed to Joseph, Mary was actually his "wife" even though they had not lived together. In the case of a maiden, the betrothal, or engagement period, lasted about a year; for widows, it lasted one month. If Joseph had died before the year of betrothal was up, Mary would have become a widow without ever having had the marriage consummated. (If you remember the discussion of levirate marriages in our session on Ruth, Mary would have become subject to that law.)

Both Luke and Matthew support the doctrine of the virgin birth of Jesus. Mark and John do not mention it, and neither does Peter in his sermons in the book of Acts or Paul in his epistles. The church has accepted this teaching by faith while recognizing that the teaching that Jesus is the Son of God rests on more evidence than the virgin birth. His whole life and subsequent death and resurrection attest to his nature and calling.

Nevertheless, regardless of the skepticism that is often expressed toward the virgin birth, the Lukan account gives it credibility. This physician, and possible companion of Paul in his travels, evidently became intrigued by the story of Jesus and determined to make his own investigation of the events of the Lord's life (Luke 1:3-4).

Mary was probably living in the city of Ephesus with the disciple John after her son's death (John 19:27). Luke may have visited her there and heard the story of the angel's visit and her child's birth from her own lips.

It's fairly safe to assume that Mary was an extraordinary young woman. She was ordinary in the sense of being part of the everyday, workaday world; extraordinary in that her life was used by God to his glory and for the salvation of all people. In spite of attempts by the historical church to ascribe special holiness to her, there is no description of special stature in the Bible.

Mary was a young woman apparently living in Nazareth, a city in Galilee, a small region in northern Palestine. Nazareth had no noteworthy features (John 1:46), and in Mary's day it was small, secluded, and not on any main highway. Ancient non-Christian sources do not mention it. Since the village lay about 1300 feet above sea level, the climate was moderate with rainful favorable to vegetation.

Daily life for dwellers in that rural setting was probably much like rural life today. Marriages were arranged at that time by family members with the help and advice of friends. Mary's betrothed was a carpenter whose trade may have brought him to Nazareth for a time.

Unexpectedly, during her year of waiting for the marriage to be finalized, Mary became pregnant. Luke tells us that an angel named Gabriel, the same messenger sent to Daniel (Dan. 9:21), was sent to inform her that she would give birth to the Son of the Most High, because she had found favor with God.

No matter how little we know about Mary up to this point, now her character, as Luke describes her, begins to unfold. She questioned the angel.

"How can this be since I'm not married?" (see Luke 1:34).

It's a perfectly natural question. Never before has a baby been conceived without a woman having intercourse with a man. That's the only way babies have been made. Is there another way?

"The Holy Spirit will come upon you . . ." (Luke 1:35).

The seal of this covenant was the pregnancy of Elizabeth, an elderly relative, who had never had a child but now in her old age was already six months pregnant.

Mary made her decision. She yielded to God's plan for her life. She did not consult Joseph or a priest or a rabbi or anyone else. We begin to see one of the traits that set her apart for a heavy assignment, her willingness to assume responsibility for her own life. Remember what we said about women as "risk takers" in our last session? Mary may just be the greatest risk taker of all time.

How often during her life was she to wonder exactly what being the "favored one" of God meant? If it meant happiness, prosperity, and freedom from pain, then she was not favored. The favor of God may not always be known in days of freedom from care, but rather in those times when faith is tested and the presence of God is revealed—in answer to our cries for deliverance.

No one has ever accused Mary of failing to live up to her commitment. She was often puzzled, yes. She was greatly troubled, she was afraid, she pondered events and sayings that she did not understand, but she stayed with this strange and wonderful son of hers.

Mary did a very human thing, however. She went "with haste" to visit her relative Elizabeth to have her faith in the angel's message reinforced. Because Elizabeth was filled with the Holy Spirit, she recognized Mary as the mother of the Christ. The angel's message was verified; Mary was blessed for her acceptance in faith of God's promise.

For Mary, life had both ended and begun. What did she suffer during these months of pregnancy? Were the townspeople cruel to her? Did she fear for her life?

As God-fearing people, her neighbors knew that she ought to be stoned to death as an adulteress (Lev. 20:10). The guilty man, too, if they could find the one who had made her pregnant. Her "husband Joseph" (Matt. 1:19) was sure she had betrayed him and wanted to divorce her quietly. God had to intervene in Joseph's dreams, says Matthew, to save Mary and her baby.

Mary's discipleship was shaped and disciplined through the years. First, Herod tried to kill the precious child by ordering all male children in Bethlehem two years and under to be put to death. Second, they almost lost Jesus on one of their Passover journeys to Jerusalem. Her sensitivity to her son's calling no doubt increased daily in hundreds of little ways. The wisdom he demonstrated in the temple (Luke 2:46-47) certainly could not be hidden at home.

The time came when she knew he had to start moving in the direction that was to lead to the cross. The gospel of John tells us that it was the "signs" Jesus did that divided the crowds into people of belief and people of unbelief. Those who chose unbelief would eventually see to it that he died for revealing signs of his divine power (John 11:47-48).

In John's gospel it was Mary who started Jesus on that fateful journey to the cross when she initiated the first of those signs, the making of water into wine at the wedding of Cana (John 2:1-11). Even though Jesus protested, "My hour has not yet come," he nevertheless responded to her request. Luke portrayed Mary unsheathing the very sword that was to pierce her own heart, as the prophet Simeon had foretold (Luke 2:35).

When that time came, John tells us that she stayed at the cross, listening to her son's cries of agony, watching his blood drop from his wounds and no doubt feeling every throbbing pain. If her presence could compensate even a little for his suffering and aloneness, she would give him that comfort.

Jesus knew she was there. "Woman, behold your son! [John] . . . Behold, your mother!" Take care of her . . . for my sake (see John 19:26-27).

It was a long journey from the angelic visit in the little village of Nazareth to the lonely hill outside Jerusalem. She who had carried him in her womb knew that the bond welded throughout a lifetime had power to nourish and sustain her.

The Summary: Women as Spirit-Filled

Mary's visit to Elizabeth was motivated by more than a desire to check on the angel's words. Any woman who has gone through a life-changing experience knows that deep longing to contact another person who has had a similar experience.

A conversion event, a crisis, a strange emotion, a new sensation, a unique encounter—all call for confirmation. We need to touch someone who will understand, someone who might hold us and say, "There, there, I know what you mean. I understand. I've been there, too."

Mary may have longed for that kind of understanding. Since the angel had mentioned Elizabeth's unique situation, then Elizabeth might be the one person in the world who wouldn't think she was crazy, or an adulteress, or a liar. Even Joseph did not believe her. That must have hurt.

Any experience that sets us apart from those around us results in a deep sense of loneliness. We can imagine Mary to be one of the loneliest persons in her world. Whenever the Holy Spirit breaks into our lives, we are in new territory. The Spirit is always present at the moment of creation, bringing into being something that has never existed before.

Throughout history, and especially since Pentecost, there have been fresh encounters with the Spirit as individuals witness to the ongoing truth about Christ (John 16:13). In recent decades the Holy Spirit has been poured out on the church in some remarkable ways. Gifts of the Spirit that had been ignored, forgotten, or assigned to the first century church have been bringing new insights to the people of God today.

It seems that the Spirit is challenging the church with new life and energy. With great power the church is growing in continents that once seemed likely to resist any significant inroads by the gospel. When we meet Christians from places where the church is under oppression and persecution, our spirits leap in response, sensing their vitality of spirit.

Mary found that kind of response in Elizabeth. This old woman who was pregnant for the first time knew intuitively what had happened to the younger woman. The Spirit in her filled her with the spirit of prophecy and discernment. Luke says that even the baby in Elizabeth's womb, six months along in his life, was filled with the Spirit and leaped in acknowledgment.

Mary was no longer lonely, no longer afraid. Opening her lips, she praised God. Luke took the words of Hannah (1 Sam. 2:1-10), words Mary had probably memorized, and made them part of Mary's song of praise (Luke 1:46-55). While praising God, she also seems to understand more clearly what impact God's action in the world is bound to have on the social order. Love and justice would inevitably topple the rich and mighty and exalt the poor and humble.

Mary stayed with Elizabeth for three months (Luke 1:56). Wouldn't you like to know what they talked about? If the Magnificat is a sample of their conversation and prayers, what a marvelous time of renewal it must have been for them both! Now Mary had strength to go back to Nazareth and face the townspeople, her family, and Joseph.

Today also, women are seeking other women in order to draw strength from each other once more. They are validating each other's experiences because they know even more than Mary and Elizabeth knew: Jesus has risen! The Spirit did not betray those two friends in their life of discipleship and suffering. The gospel writers indicate that everything came to pass as the angel had said it would.

We have much to share with each other. None of us needs to walk alone. We have the Spirit and we have each other. And Emmanuel, Son of God and child of Mary, is with us.

Questions for Reflection

1. Zechariah, Mary, and the shepherds all had the same reaction to the appearance of the angel (Luke 1:12,29-30; 2:9). Why do you think their reaction was one of fear?

2. The phrase "filled with the Holy Spirit" appears several times in Luke 1. What is its meaning in the context of this chapter?

3. How does Mary describe God in her song of praise, the "Magnificat?" How do you feel about her description?

4. Luke 2:41-51 says something about the relationship of Jesus with his "parents." Joseph is called Jesus' "father" by Mary and she did not seem to understand her son's reference to his "Father's" business. What do you understand about this?

5. Often tradition has pictured Mary as a passive vessel, a woman who simply accepted what happened. After studying the Bible text, would you agree with this portrait? What qualities of deep spirituality did Mary exhibit? What is the difference between passive resignation and active acceptance?

11

John 4:1-30
(Supplementary texts: Luke 7:11-17, 36-50; 8:43-48, 49-56;
10:38-42; 13:10-13; 21:1-4)

THE SAMARITAN
WOMAN

The Setting: From Jerusalem to Galilee

If you have been faithfully reading this book, you are aware that Jesus established some new patterns of behavior with women. You realize also that some of the things you have been told that the Bible says about women do not find their basis in the life and teachings of Jesus but rather in the writings of the apostle Paul who was charged with the establishment of congregations after Jesus' death and resurrection.

Paul had the difficult task of bringing the good news into both Jewish and Gentile settings. He had been "educated according to the strict manner of the law of our fathers" (Acts 22:3), a Jew who was "a Pharisee, a son of Pharisees" (Acts 23:6), a tradition that did not permit men to speak to women in public, not even their wives.

This man struggled with the tensions between his own traditions and the newness he had experienced through faith in the risen Jesus. So in one of his earliest writings, the letter to the Galatians, he testified to the freedom from the law that all believers know through Jesus. Without equivocation he says,

For as many of you as were baptized into Christ have put on Christ. There is neither Jew nor Greek, there is neither slave nor free, there is neither male nor female; for you are all one in Christ Jesus (Gal. 3:27-28).

In response to specific congregational problems, however, Paul often went back to Hebrew traditions to maintain order. One of those traditions demanded the silence of women in church meetings (1 Cor. 14:34). He asked wives to be subject to their husbands in the letter to the Ephesians (Eph. 5:24), but since he knew that in Christ there is no distinction between males and females, he prefaces that section of the letter with the mutual subjection of husband and wife to each other "out of reverence for Christ" (Eph. 5:21).

Women must go to the Gospels to understand who they are as followers of Jesus. There we meet a person who was totally able to establish friendships and partnerships with women, completely accepting them as whole persons. As God in the flesh, he knew that women and men were both created in the "image of God" (Gen. 1:27), and he understood all of them thoroughly.

In this session, we are going to discover our Lord in one of the unique encounters recorded in the Gospels. We find him in conversation with a woman, the longest conversation with either man or woman of which we have record.

He was on his way to Galilee from Jerusalem. Because Jews and Samaritans were divided by religious differences, it was customary for Jews to avoid going through Samaria, a country lying between Judea and Galilee. In order to skirt that country when traveling north from Jerusalem, Jews would make a detour east across the Jordan River and only go west again when they were north of Samaria. (Look at a map in the back of your Bible or find a Bible atlas in your church library.)

In our study of John's account of Jesus' encounter with a woman in Samaria, we are going to unlearn some of the traditional interpretations that have been repeated over and over again by preachers and teachers. Most have seen her through their own masculine eyes and have convinced us that she must be cast in the role of a sinful woman.

But Jesus intentionally sought her out. We are going to probe into the record and ask Why *this particular woman?* What was there about her that made Jesus lead his disciples through a country they despised so he could talk to her at length in the hottest part of the day? There were many sinful men and women in Jerusalem and Galilee. If he only wanted to expose sin, he didn't have to go so far out of his way. Why then this woman?

What made the apostle John, the beloved friend of Jesus, remember this particular incident and want to write it down for the historical record? We may not answer all of these questions, but we will try to discover what it was that made the Samaritan woman so special to Jesus and to John.

The Story: The Rejected Woman

(This section is based on the Bible account, scholarly sources, and personal reflection. Let your imagination help you re-create the Samaritan woman and her encounter with Jesus.)

The fact that the Scripture tells us that Jesus was very intentional about having to go through Samaria (John 4:4, translated by the King James Version as "he must needs go through Samaria," emphasizing his determination to journey by this undesirable route) informs us at the very outset of the story that his meeting with the woman at the well was no accident. He who knew all things and read the hidden secrets of the heart intended to meet her.

Jesus always went out of his way to confront those who had reached the limit of human endurance—Jairus, a ruler of the synagogue (Luke 8:40-56), and the widow of Nain (Luke 7:11-17) both lost their only children; the woman with the issue of blood making her a social outcast for 12 years (Luke 8:43-48); the woman whose back was bent for 18 years so that she could not straighten up (Luke 13:10-17)—all were desperate people singled out by Jesus for special ministry.

Had the woman of Samaria reached the limit of her endurance? Let's examine the reason she came alone to that well at noonday. It seems doubtful that she came because she was such a sinner that she avoided people by coming at an hour when no one else came. Were there no other sinners in Samaria? If she were as brazen as many interpreters of this passage indicated, then she certainly would not shun other women. Brazen people flaunt their sins.

What did Jesus see in her that others did not see? On this particular day Jesus saw a woman in need. Perhaps she was ready to give up, perhaps take her own life. We can only guess. Was she a sinner, or, just possibly, had she been sinned against?

The critical moment in their conversation came when Jesus told her to call her husband (4:16). "I have no husband," she said. Was that a confession of sin or a statement of repeated rejection?

You will recall that women in that mideast culture could not divorce their husbands, and if they committed adultery they would be stoned. Samaritans honored the Pentateuch, the first five books of the Bible, as the permanent and immutable word of God given to Moses. Therefore, Samaritans would be as strict as Jews in their observance of Deut. 24:1-4, which says,

> "When a man takes a wife and marries her, if then she finds no favor in his eyes because he has found some indecency in her, and he writes her a bill of divorce and puts it in her hand and sends her out of his house, and she departs out of his house, and if she goes and becomes another man's wife, and the latter husband dislikes her and writes her a bill of divorce and puts it in her hand and sends her out of his house, or if the latter husband dies, who took her to be his wife, then her former husband, who sent her away, may not take her again to be his wife, after she has been defiled. . . ."

A woman could be sent away by a husband if she did anything to displease him. "Indecency" might be burning the barley cakes! Perhaps her only sin as a woman was not being pretty, or not being a good cook, or not being able to manipulate a man.

If her first husband had died, she may have been passed on to his brother to bear children for him as in the Levirate marriage (Deut. 25:5-10) we discussed in the session on Ruth. But what if she couldn't bear children? What other life was there for a woman who had no supportive and loving husband in those days?

Rejection brings the severest of all pains, especially when that rejection comes from someone to whom we have given our love. Since women could not divorce their husbands and since being an adulteress would have caused her to be stoned, where did anyone ever get the idea that the Samaritan woman was a sinner? She was not a prostitute or she would not have had husbands.

She was a woman who had been rejected, divorced, and put out of the house by five husbands, most likely because she could not bear children. Her simple answer, "I have no husband," revealed to Jesus all of her pain, the pain of unrequited love. Jesus, of all people, could identify with that pain. John wrote about that. "He came to his own home, and his own people received him not" (John 1:11). He was "despised and rejected by men . . . as one from whom men hide their faces . . ." (Isa. 53:3).

Yes, Jesus knew her pain. Her loneliness at that well was comparable to his sense of forsakenness on the cross. He reached out to her, perhaps the first word of acceptance she had heard for a long, long time. And when she begins to tell him about herself, he says, "I know. I know all about your five husbands and your present situation. I know that you are speaking the truth." That's all. No word of condemnation, just understanding. "I know what it feels like not to be wanted, to be treated with contempt by people you were willing to love and serve," his voice seemed to say to her.

Many have said her change in the direction of the conversation was an attempt to hide behind religion, to avoid more self-revelation. Was it? Or was it the response that always comes from someone who has been treated with dignity? She recognized that Jesus was no ordinary traveler and longed to continue this conversation with the insightful and compassionate stranger. Hiding behind God-talk? No, rather she was plunging right into the only thing that had sustained her all through those aching years of rejection, her faith in the coming Messiah.

"I am he," says Jesus, revealing to her something he had not revealed to anyone else, the most unequivocal statement of his identity as the promised Savior.

When the disciples return, they cannot believe that he is talking to a woman. Do you see how different Jesus was? He treated women as equals, worthy in every way to receive his deepest truths. The disciples did not even see that he was changing the world for women, defying religious and cultural norms that place them in an inferior position.

"God is a Spirit," Jesus told the woman, "keep on worshiping God in spirit and in truth."

Life for the woman at the well was changed forever! She was no longer the "rejected one," she was accepted, loved, forgiven, lifted up, worthy! She left that symbol of her old life, her water pot, and ran to the nearby town of Sychar to tell everybody she met about the man at the well.

When your life has been changed by Jesus, everyone you meet is going to recognize the difference. No matter what the townspeople had felt about her before, they now believed what she said. She was the "sower" who planted the seeds of evangelism for the later "harvest" that Jesus was telling his disciples about (John 4:35-38). He affirmed her as an evangelist, testifying that her witness was valid and was bearing fruit even as he and the disciples were talking.

Did she go back to the man she was living with? We don't know. But if she did, you can be sure their relationship changed as a result of her new sense of value, and her new testimony. Jesus had to go through Samaria—for her sake and for the sake of Samaria.

The Summary: Women as Seekers

The New Testament has recorded enough stories of women who were confronted by Jesus or who reached out to him to give us a very clear picture of his attitude and behavior toward them. No wonder that many women came seeking him. From him they received understanding and a love they had never experienced from the formal religionists of their day.

Luke tells about some of them. In Luke 7:36-50, Jesus has no words of condemnation for a woman who is labeled "a sinner." We are not told what her sin was but are led to believe that she was a prostitute. She came to the house where Jesus had been invited to dinner by Simon the Pharisee.

What powerful attraction did Jesus have that could make a woman dare to enter the house of a Pharisee? The word perhaps had gotten around that this man treated women in some new ways. He was a man who was at home with, and respecting of, women, a most unusual combination.

So the woman came seeking him. She offended the Pharisee by anointing Jesus' feet, wiping them with the hair of her head and kissing them while he lay on the couch eating.

Jesus gave her what she was seeking—forgiveness and a new start in life.

A new start in life! Isn't that what we receive from Jesus? Luke tells about a woman who had been hemorrhaging vaginally for 12 years (Luke 8:43-48). She came because she had not been able to sleep in the same bed with her husband, she couldn't touch him or her children (if she still had a husband and children); she could have no social contacts because if anyone touched her they would be unclean (Lev. 15:25-28). For 12 long years!

She dared to touch Jesus, longing for healing, for a new start in life. Jesus accepted and affirmed her touch, denying her uncleanness, forever repudiating that a woman could be unclean because of her bodily discharges.

Rejection as a reality for women today

So many women today are feeling rejected. They have been divorced, deserted, or told they are not loved any more by the men to whom they gave their love and their lives. Divorces after two or more decades of marriage are becoming commonplace.

Somehow, it's still often suggested that it must be the woman's "fault" when her husband abandons her. Sometimes it may be, but more often she is simply discarded for a younger woman. In addition to the suffocating sense of being personally unwanted and unloved, these women may even find their church rejecting them. Just when they need love and friendship, they are shunned and left out of social gatherings.

We are called to follow the example of Jesus. The Gospels record no instance where Jesus turned a woman away when she came seeking his favor. In fact, he seems to go out of his way to make even the most disreputable women feel loved (John 8:3-11). Jesus sees women as the victims of male-dominated religion and society, and he reminds us in both word and deed that this is not God's will for their lives. They, too, have been called to "hear the word of God and keep it!" (Luke 11:28).

Loneliness as a prelude to new life

As it was for the woman at the well, a period of loneliness and rejection may be also a time of creative newness. Forced to search for new relationships and new resources for coping with rejection and the bitterness of abandonment, one turns to the Spirit for counsel and comfort.

Just when it seems that all is lost and there is no light at the end of the tunnel, the Lord meets women at the well and says, "I know. I understand. God's around."

Like the woman at the well, we can drop the water pots of our old lives, our rejections, our loneliness, our despairs, and run with our lives. We have found the water of life and will never thirst again!

Questions for Reflection

1. Does it make any difference to you to learn that Jesus got tired?

2. In John 4:7-12, the woman's remarks have a brittle, sarcastic edge to them. How did your reading of "the rejected woman" help you to understand why she might sound this way?

3. When have you experienced Jesus as "living water?" (Note how Jesus turns a very ordinary conversation into an intimate and re- vealing communication.) What dry and thirsty areas of your life did he water?

4. Jews did not consider women or Samaritans worthy of theological dialog, yet in John 4:19-26 Jesus speaks earnestly and in depth with a Samaritan woman. Is there anyone you consider as a "Samaritan and a woman" and thus incapable of comprehending spiritual things? Would you invite them to your church? Have you ever been treated this way?

12

Luke 10:38-42; John 11:1-44; 12:1-11

MARTHA

A Home Away from Home

Everyone needs a home, a place of belonging. Jesus was no exception. Let's examine some of the reasons why he found in the home of Martha, Mary, and their brother Lazarus a place of warmth and welcome, a home away from home. In the loving relationship he shared with them, Jesus found the family he needed to sustain him during his years of public ministry.

The gospels give no evidence of a close relationship between Jesus and his half-brothers and sisters. In fact there was a time when some of the folks in a crowd that had gathered around him called Jesus' attention to the fact that his mother and brothers were outside asking for him (Mark 3:31-35).

Instead of rushing eagerly to greet them, Jesus asked a strange question, "Who are my mother and my brothers?" He answered his own question by saying, "Whoever does the will of God is my brother, and sister, and mother."

When we investigate possible reasons for this seeming estrangement, we note that shortly before that event in the Markan narrative an incident occurs that might give us a clue to the attitude of his family toward Jesus. He was gaining a reputation as a healer, an exorcist, a breaker of Sabbath laws, and as the leader of a new sect.

This worried the religious leaders, of course, so they attacked Jesus, saying that he was himself possessed by Beelzebul, the "prince of demons" (Mark 3:22). Mark tells us that "when his family heard it, they went out to seize him, for people were saying, 'He is beside himself' " (3:21). Their motive may have been to protect him, but their actions revealed a lack of understanding of Jesus' calling and mission. Even unwittingly they became obstacles to the fulfillment of his purposes.

Perhaps their actions reveal a deeper rift in their relationship with this unusual son and brother. His mother undoubtedly knew what he was doing but may have been trying to postpone the day when the "sword" prophesied by Simeon (Luke 2:35) would pierce her own soul. The brothers and sisters, however, may have been embarrassed by their brother's actions and suffered harassment because of them. After all, it would be rather difficult to believe that one's very own brother could be doing such unusual things and still be sane!

If Jesus no longer felt accepted by his own brothers and sisters and was denied an enthusiastic welcome in their homes, there were those who saw beyond his human form and recognized him as the One he claimed to be. Mary, Martha, and Lazarus—his "adopted" sisters and brother—accepted him as the true human being he was while at the same time seeing the One he was beyond that human form. With them he found the "home" where he was accepted without reservation, a place of love and normal, everyday conversation. In their home he could debate issues and find loving criticism and open affirmation.

Jesus was often misunderstood. Paul wrote about his own lack of comprehension in his second letter to the Corinthians (5:15ff.). Once, Paul wrote, we regarded Christ from a worldly perspective, or according to the flesh. But then Paul's life was forever changed by the Christ who grabbed him on his murderous journey to Damascus and made him a "new creature." From that point on, Paul looked at the whole world and all people through his new eyes and with his new eyesight.

Martha saw Jesus with that same clear-sightedness. She apparently owned the house that she shared with her sister and brother (Luke 10:38), and John tells us that "Jesus loved Martha and her sister and Lazarus" (John 11:5). She understood the ministry of hospitality without which early Christian evangelists could not have established the many missions they did. We have the impression that Martha's goal as a hostess was to make her guests as comfortable as possible. Perhaps she was too concerned. Sometimes guests prefer just to sit, relax, and even just to stare into space. However she practiced hospitality, we have no doubt that for Martha, "my home is your home"—*mi casa es su casa.*

John 11:18 tells us that Bethany, Martha's hometown, was "near Jerusalem, about two miles off." Mark adds that it was "at the Mount of Olives" on the eastern slope as one travels from Jericho (Mark 11:1).

The Story: The Lady of the House

(This section is based on the Bible account, scholarly sources, and personal reflection. Let your imagination help you re-create Martha's experience.)

We are separating the stories of Martha and Mary in order that we may appreciate these sisters as individuals. Too often they are treated as Siamese twins. They are not exceptions to the fact that every woman is a unique human being whose gifts are needed by the Christian community and by society. Martha's gifts must not be overlooked. Like all the rest of us, she is a complex personality and cannot be identified with simple definitions.

History and preaching have too often ignored Martha's multifaceted personality by describing her as a fussy, complaining housekeeper. Martha's name may more accurately describe her. Her name is the Aramaic form for "lady" or "mistress," with "lady" being the feminine form of "lord." She owned her own home and as such was the head of a household, presiding over land and servants. No mention is made of marriage for Martha or her brother and sister. They just all lived together, and Martha seemed to be in charge. She took that responsibility seriously.

"Martha was distracted with much serving," Luke tells us (10:40). The Greek word used here for "serving" (*diakonia*) is the same one translated in other New Testament contexts as "ministry" or "service," specifically the exercise of liturgical and serving functions in the church. Luke, the writer of both the Gospel and of the Acts of the Apostles, uses the word in this context also in Acts 1:17,25; 6:1,4; 11:29; 12:25; 20:24; and 21:19. Only in this reference to Martha in Luke 10:40 has the Greek word been interpreted by the writers of Greek lexicons (dictionaries) as referring to domestic duties.

The writer of The Gospel According to John, however, views Martha in the role of "server" (again the same word as the one used for the service of deacons and ministers) at a supper given for Jesus and his disciples (John 12:2). Whether or not she was acting as a forerunner of the deacons who served later in the Johannine community and as Luke identified them in Acts 6, she was assuming a role not given to women in the orthodox Jewish community. Women were not permitted to be present at male gatherings.

We who take for granted social gatherings of both men and women are not prepared to think of Martha as doing anything out of the ordinary. In fact we are more likely to think of her as fulfilling women's "traditional" role. Instead we need to see her actions as part of that startling newness that Jesus brought into the life of women and men. Earnestness of conversation and friendship are characteristic of his relationship with women. When John tells us that Jesus changed the master/servant role to that of "friend," we find a clue to his treatment of other persons. A *friend*, he tells us, is one who knows everything the other person knows. Nothing is hidden or held back, unlike the *servant* ("slave" is the root meaning of the Greek word in John 15:15) who "does not know what his master is doing."

In Jesus' dealings with his followers, friendly openness prevails. No pretense, no coyness, no subtleties. All he asks in return is the same integrity of response.

Martha responded in that way. When she complained, as Luke tells us, about Jesus' seeming lack of concern that she was left with all of the domestic work while he engaged her sister in conversation (Luke 10:40), Martha was so sure of his complete acceptance of her as a friend that she even ordered him to tell Mary to help her!

From our historical perspective 19 centuries later, her boldness is unbelievable. The passive role assigned to women in following centuries is completely out of keeping with her actions.

John's gospel ascribes an active leadership role in the community around Jesus to Martha. Her brother became very ill. Naturally the sisters sent for the one whom they valued as a friend but whom they also recognized as having more than ordinary powers. Jesus did not come before their brother died even though he had more than enough time to respond.

This kind of treatment from one who had been like a brother himself and who had told her many times that he loved her (John 11:5) seemed an affront to friendship. Martha was not one to pretend everything was all right when she didn't feel that way. When she was informed that Jesus was finally in Bethany and on his way to their house, she didn't sit in the house, seething with anger or pouting, but she went out and met him on the way with the words, "Lord, if you had been here, my brother would not have died" (John 11:21). Was there a hint of accusation in her words, or was she simply stating a fact? We don't know, of course, but the fact that her sister later repeated the same words (v. 32) indicates that they may have agreed to let Jesus know how they felt about his delay.

Jesus did not tell her that she "shouldn't feel that way." He accepted her feelings as a valid human response. He did not chide her or tell her to be silent. We really don't know what Martha expected of Jesus since her brother was already dead when she said to him, "and even now I know that whatever you ask from God, God will give you" (John 11:22). What power had she seen in him? Was she aware that he had returned Jairus' 12-year-old daughter to life when she had died (Luke 8:52-55)? Had she heard about the dead son of the widow of Nain being restored to life (Luke 7:11-17)? The report of that event had gone all over Judea, we are told. Besides, both of these life-restoring episodes had happened in response to the needs of women. Martha may have reasoned that perhaps—yes, just perhaps—Jesus might be moved to do the same for them.

That trembling hope was strengthened by Jesus' response, "Your brother will rise again" (John 11:23). Again we must note that he dealt with Martha in the same way he dealt with the Samaritan woman—as a person of intelligence and spiritual perception. Even though she did not yet dare to hope for an immediate return of her brother to life, she explored with him the implications of his words by venturing her own perceptions and understanding of the resurrection-theology of her day. She expressed the position of those who, like the Pharisees, believed in the resurrection of the dead (in contrast to the Sadducees who did not believe, Acts 23:7-8).

Jesus affirmed her response and gave her the most direct statement of his resurrection that we find in the Gospels, "I am the resurrection and the life . . ." (John 11:25). This statement reminds us again of the direct affirmation of messiahship given to the Samaritan woman when she engaged him in theological dialog.

The fact that all of their conversation took place while they were walking along a public road is in itself a remarkable thing since Jewish men did not carry on public conversations with women. In this case Jesus' entire traveling party and the villagers who were mourning Lazarus' death had to wait while Jesus and Martha talked (John 11:30).

The entire entourage probably came to a complete stop as Martha made her confession of faith, "Yes, Lord; I believe that you are the Christ, the Son of God, he who is coming into the world" (John 11:27). At one time, we are told by Matthew, Peter made the exact same confession (16:16). The Greek words are identical in the two gospel texts.

Her confession of saving faith told Jesus that she was satisfied that he was in charge. She was assured that out of his identity as the "Son of God" he would do what was right for her family. Faith is always the matrix from which new life is born. Martha left Jesus and hurried back home to tell her sister that Jesus also wanted to see her.

If Luke gives us a picture of sisterly rivalry and sibling jealousy, John dispels that notion. The sisters worked in harmony. In the first part of Chapter 11, we see this unity in verse three. Both sisters sent for Jesus and agreed on the words of the message, "Lord, he whom you love is ill."

Now, when Mary went to Jesus in response to Martha's request, she also, as we have noted above, said the same words to him. The sisters were, in this situation, "one in the Spirit."

At the tomb where the whole community had gathered, it was Martha who again addressed Jesus. She who had just so eloquently expressed her faith in the one whom she had, in true apostolic confession, perceptively identified as "the Christ, the Son of God," now revealed her human doubts in his ability. She and Peter showed the same style of leadership. She, like Peter, who denied the Lord three times even after he had made his confession of Jesus' true identity, now wavered in her faith.

"Lord," she protested, "by this time there will be an odor, for he has been dead four days." The flesh is decaying; do we really want to see the corpse? Do we want to smell the stench of death? Martha may not even have been sure that she wanted her prayers answered at this point. What would it mean to have a dead, decaying brother brought back to life? Would he be the same as he used to be? Would Lazarus be damaged, different, no longer the brother they knew?

But Jesus *loved* Martha. That meant that he would never do anything that would violate her faith. For a while it may have appeared that something dreadful and unexpected was about to happen, but Martha's fears were dispelled when she was reminded by Jesus, "Did I not tell you that if you would believe you would see the glory of God?"

That's exactly what Martha and all the rest of the crowd saw! When Jesus called his name, her brother emerged from the tomb, the bandages and grave cloths were removed, and Lazarus was very much alive and in their world again. He was their very same brother, restored to wholeness, the fresh glow of health on his cheeks.

The supper described in John 12:1-2 would appear to be their celebrative response to Lazarus' Great Event. When Jesus returned to Bethany shortly before the last week of his life, Martha organized and served a supper for him. Her faith had been honored by Jesus in Lazarus' restoration. The scene was set in her home for another remarkable episode in the life of Jesus. But we will have to wait for the story of her sister to find out about that.

The Summary: Women as Sisters

How few sister relationships are revealed in the Bible! There are many brother stories—Cain and Abel, Jacob and Esau, all of the

sons of Jacob, Moses and Aaron, James and John, Peter and An-
drew—too many to name. But how many sister stories are there?
Very few.

Where women are identified as sisters, it's usually in relationship
to a father, brother, lover, or in the New Testament in relation to
another Christian worker. Remember Abraham and Sarah? He wanted her to pretend to be his sister so that Abimelech and the Pharaoh
(in different episodes) would not kill him in order to make Sarah
one of their wives. According to the story, you recall, she was so
beautiful even as an older woman that men found her very desirable.
But that doesn't tell us anything about true sisterhood.

In the Song of Solomon, the aggressive woman lover is referred
to by her beloved as "my sister" (Song of Sol. 4:9ff.), but this represents a meaning quite foreign to our understanding of that relationship.

Jesus, we are told, had sisters as well as brothers, but we are told
nothing about their interactions with him or with each other. In fact,
we know the names of his brothers but not of his sisters.

The relationships of women are not considered important in the
Bible. Where women are identified as siblings, it is always as daughters and not as sisters. Moses, for instance, was fleeing from justice
after he had murdered an Egyptian when he met the seven daughters
of the priest of Midian, one of whom he later married. We are given
no clues about their life together as sisters. They are to remain in
the record only as "daughters."

The daughters of Zelophehad

But then there are the "daughters of Zelophehad." Although never
identified by their sister relationship, these five sisters are actually
named in the Bible, probably because of their unusual action in
demanding an inheritance of part of their father's property. They
are "Mahlah, Noah, Hoglah, Milcah, and Tirzah" (Num. 27:1).

Did these women make the first demand for equal rights? Is that
why they're remembered? The request the five sisters made was
perfectly reasonable but, for their time, very radical. You recall that,
in a patriarchal society, women could not inherit property. Only sons

were inheritors. The daughters of Zelophehad had no brothers, however, so the five sisters agreed on a course of action. How often does this happen, do you think?

Here is what they wanted. "And they stood before Moses, and before Eleazar the priest, and before the leaders and all the congregation" (quite an impressive array of male leadership!) and stated their case. "Our father," they said, "died in the wilderness . . . and he had no sons. Why should the name of our father be taken away from his family, because he had no son? Give to us a possession among our father's brethren" (Num. 27:2-4). In a rather complicated response to their plea, Moses nevertheless agreed that the "daughters of Zelophehad are right: you shall give them possession of an inheritance among their father's brethren and cause the inheritance of their father to pass to them" (27:7).

In this case only blood sisters could have effected a change in the law. Which one of them first expressed this radical idea? How much protest did the others raise? Were they frightened? Did they pray together before they went in to the leaders? Were they praised for their actions or did people see them as troublemakers and revolutionaries? We cherish their memory because they demonstrate the kind of changes women can make in the histories of their families and of the wider society through their own sister ties and unity of purpose.

Conflict and intimacy

The relationship of Martha and Mary is rare indeed, for theirs reveals sister interaction in a way found nowhere else in the Scriptures. Mary can refuse to assume her responsibility as cohostess with her sister; Martha can be frustrated and irritated with her sister and complain about her to a friend. At the same time, we see them exchanging leadership roles gracefully, deferring to each other in public, and appearing to think with one mind while they maintain independence and autonomy.

If there was rivalry between them, it seemed to arise from their calling as disciples that motivated them to want the best for Jesus. Martha wanted his needs met in the way in which she was most comfortable, and Mary fulfilled her vocation in the manner which best suited her. Both were trying to "outdo one another in showing honor" to Jesus. They seemed to be of one spirit in that desire.

Sisterhood, as demonstrated by Martha and Mary, allows each one's gifts to be identified and used in ministry. Sometimes that involves conflict as roles are examined, affirmed or rejected, or changed. Conflict is a part of life and must be confronted if life is to move on and change to meet a changing world.

Conflict can be viewed as harmful, like a disease, or as the natural result of closeness. If we adopt the medical model, we will see it as something to be treated and cured. But if we understand it as the friction that occurs when two objects or persons are in close working contact, then it can be accepted as the natural outcome of intimacy. Any two people who live and work in close daily contact are bound to rub each other the wrong way at times.

Our need, as sisters, is to learn how to deal with conflict so that it can lead us to greater understanding and closeness and not to alienation and separation.

Fortunate are the women who have a blood sister and who know how to build on that relationship. If blood sisters are not part of our history, then we can find close ties with our spiritual sisters. In either case we are learning how to relate to each other as "sisters" as well as "daughters."

Questions for Reflection

1. In what ways can you identify with Martha as a homemaker and head of household?

2. What emotions are aroused in you by the rebuke Jesus gives to Martha? Can you recall any time in your life when such a rebuke might have been given to you?

3. What do you learn about stereotyping of individual women from the accounts of Martha's encounters with Jesus? Think of the women you know as excellent housekeepers. Then think of them in some of their other roles. What new appreciations of them did you gain from Martha?

4. How do you react to Martha? Does she remind you of anyone you know? Do you see yourself in her?

5. Martha's moment of doubt at the tomb (John 11:39) after her strong confession reminds us again that "low" moments often follow our "peak" experiences. When have you noticed this sort of reaction in your own life?

13

Luke 10:38-42; John 11:1-44; 12:1-11

MARY OF BETHANY

In the House of Bread

Meanwhile, back in Bethany ("house of bread"), we need to become acquainted with Mary, the other sister, also beloved by Jesus (John 11:5).

While Martha comes across as a straightforward, honest, and easily understood person in Scripture, Mary seems cloaked in mystery. Who is this woman whom the gospel writers found so fascinating and whom they surrounded with a variety of reports? Veiled in her own persona, her motives and actions are hidden in a historical secret like the secret hidden behind the smile of the *Mona Lisa*.

One thing we know for certain about her. She was hungry for the Bread of Life. She understood what Jesus meant when he was talking to the crowds who followed him looking for more "loaves" (John 6:26). They "murmured at him, because he said, 'I am the bread which came down from heaven' " (6:41), but Mary had an insatiable craving for that bread of life that alone could satisfy her hunger.

Although her usual role was to take her place beside her sister in the preparation and serving of food (otherwise her sister would not have complained that Mary had "left" her to serve alone), she would tolerate no obstacle to the fulfillment of her driving passion. She would indeed eat of that "bread" without which her spirit would starve to death no matter how many meals she prepared and served!

She seemed oblivious to (or ignored) the fact that Jesus and his followers had traveled hot, dusty roads and were waiting to eat. They were hungry people hoping for solid Jewish bread with enough calories to fuel body and spirit for many demanding tasks. It's doubtful that Jesus was there alone. At least the 12 men who traveled with him (Mark 3:14-19) and all the women who journeyed with him (Luke 8:2-3) would have been there with him.

No wonder Martha complained when her sister abdicated her helping role. In a day when fast foods were unobtainable and refrigeration an improbable luxury, preparation of food was a full-time task. A woman could truthfully say, "I've been slaving over a hot stove all day!" Even a meal of bread alone required long hours of preparation from the grinding of grains to the baking on hot stones (1 Kings 19:6), in an oven, or on a griddle (Lev. 2:4-5).

Although the biblical record indicates that Martha and her siblings were not poor and could afford to entertain guests at dinner (both Luke and John tell us about their dinner parties) and could perhaps hire servants to do some of the meal preparation, their closeness to Jesus would perhaps not call for such formality. The occasion in Luke is surely a family gathering with close friends.

The supper which served as a setting in John 12:1-8 appeared to be a more formal occasion described by the phrase "they made him a supper" (12:2) as being in Jesus' honor. Some see Luke's account of the dinner at the home of Simon the Pharisee (7:36-50) and Mark's version of the dinner at the house of Simon the leper in Bethany as referring to the same occasion as John describes in 12:1-8.

The Story: The Anointer

(This section is based on the Bible account, scholarly sources, and personal reflection. Let your imagination help you re-create Mary's experience.)

How does one tell the story of a woman who says very little and appears rather passive but whose few actions are so vigorously championed by Jesus? Mystery certainly surrounds her, and we are left to much speculation in our attempts to analyze meanings behind these actions.

First of all, we meet her in Luke's gospel sitting at the feet of Jesus. Nothing in her manner suggests rebellion or impertinence. She seems simply to be oblivious to what was going on around her and to be deeply involved with what Jesus was saying. If there is any objection in the other guests to her position as a woman sitting at the feet of a rabbi (the place reserved for male students), she was unaware of it. If people were hungry and waiting for a meal to be served, she did not notice. If her sister was getting upset with her and speaking her name, her ears were tuned to another frequency.

Mary was with Jesus in that wilderness where one learns to feed on "every word that proceeds from the mouth of God" (Matt. 4:4). That's all that there was in her world.

One senses that she was not seeking permission to do what she was doing from Jesus or anyone else. She was not looking for anyone's approval any more than she was aware of disapproval. When Jesus was talking to the Samaritan woman and the disciples came and urged him to eat, his reply was that he had "food to eat of which you do not know" (John 4:32). Now Mary experienced the same phenomenon. She was being fed with the "bread of life."

Perhaps Martha was not so much irritated with Mary as she was envious of her. Martha, too, loved Jesus and knew what he had to give to those who "hunger and thirst for righteousness" (Matt. 5:6). She was caught in the conflict experienced by multitudes of women in the centuries following her. How does one decide between duty and one's heart's desire?

Martha chose duty; Mary followed the desire of her heart. Jesus rebuked Martha and commended Mary. Somehow that doesn't seem fair, does it? We who have been brought up with stern admonitions to finish our vegetables before we eat the dessert, told to get our homework done before we watch television, told to do the dusting and the dishes before we sit down to read a book, we have a hard time appreciating the word of approval given to Mary. "Mary," we would rather scoldingly remind her, "don't you know that duty comes before pleasure?"

The scolding word came from Jesus, but, surprisingly, it came to Martha! "Martha, Martha, you are anxious and troubled about many things; one thing is needful. Mary has chosen the good portion, which shall not be taken away from her" (Luke 10:41-42). Mary was not only affirmed and supported in her action; she was lifted up as a model for women in the years to come.

The rediscovery of Jesus' pledge to Mary has been an enormous encouragement to women who have longed to be part of a community of scholars dedicated to the study of God and God's revelation. For the women around Jesus this was a privilege they had never known. Forbidden to study the Torah and denied the seat of learning at the feet of the rabbis, they nevertheless knew the cry of the heart for God, that enormous hunger for the Bread which is real life. Conversation that never focuses on issues arising out of that soul's hunger becomes wearisome. To never be able to share what the heart has heard and seen of God leads to the death of the soul. To have one's thoughts as a woman trivialized and belittled is to experience spiritual abuse.

The words of Jesus fall on our hungry hearts like manna and living water. This is what it means to be loved by Jesus! To be able to speak and be answered, to have permission to say what is on one's mind and be listened to, and to be affirmed and to be encouraged in one's speaking—this is being loved!

Centuries passed and the promise of Jesus was not enforced by the church. Instead, the privilege of sitting at the feet of Jesus as student and disciple was taken away. Now, as women are being admitted to seminaries for the study of theology and being ordained to the ministries of many Protestant churches, the promise of Jesus to Mary is beginning to be restored to all of the Marys who know this to be their call to vocation.

Mary of Bethany would probably be classified as an "introvert" today; she turned to the Spirit within when she needed more strength to face the events of her life. When her brother became ill, she agreed to send for Jesus, but when he died she retreated into her own source of strength.

What did she think about when Jesus did not come to Bethany as soon as he was sent for? How could she reconcile the love she knew he felt for them and his seeming indifference to the seriousness of the situation? How could she avoid a sense of betrayal when they had all been so close?

When she heard that Jesus had finally arrived in Bethany, Mary stayed at home and let her sister go off alone to meet him. It was not her way to meet a situation head-on or to confront someone directly. That was Martha's way, not hers. We can be sure that Mary was in great pain, suffering deeply. The healthier way to deal with our hurts, we assume, is to talk about them, to lance the wound before the entire system is poisoned.

Mary appeared to be immobilized by her grief. Even her neighbors were in the house with her, consoling her (John 11:31). Her tears would not stop flowing, and even when she got up in response to her sister's command, they assumed that she was going to the tomb of her brother to continue her weeping. Was her suffering more intense because she felt some rejection on the part of Jesus?

When she confronted him, she spoke the exact words spoken by Martha, but they brought an entirely different response from Jesus. With Martha, he began a theological discussion; with Mary, "he was deeply moved in the spirit and troubled" (John 11:33). What was there about her and her weeping friends that moved him to the same awesome anguish that he later on experienced in Gethsemane (John 12:27)? Luke tells us that Jesus wept on one other occasion, when he drew near to Jerusalem on the day of his triumphal entry and knew that soon that city in which he had revealed himself as the Messiah would soon see him crucified (Luke 19:41). Perhaps Mary, whose devotion and love he could not doubt, provoked a more profound weeping than even Jerusalem could do. Jerusalem would reject him and be lost. Its suffering would be because of its unbelief. But Mary loved him and yet she, too, would have to suffer in this world because sin and death bring their pain and sorrow to all, good or bad. His pain echoed the cry, "Why do the righteous suffer?" or "Why do bad things happen to good people?"

Do you also find yourself, too, asking, "Since he could have kept Lazarus from dying and spared his friends all this pain, why did Jesus wait to come to Bethany?" Friends of the Bethany family were wondering the same thing when they asked each other, "Could not he who opened the eyes of the blind man have kept this man from dying?" (John 11:37). Mary, however, remained silent. She could only weep. She thought she knew him so well, but it seemed she did not know him at all. They were friends, but in some ways even friends remain a mystery to each other.

One of the mysterious excitements of friendship is to know another person for many years, perhaps decades, and to delight in the surprise of new discoveries. Was Jesus surprised by Mary's later response to him, when they were all at the supper the "resurrected" brother and sisters "made him" (John 12:2)? Did the raising of her brother from his tomb give Mary some prophetic insights into the next week's events? Was it a foreshadowing of the tomb of Jesus? Did she see their supper as a last supper with him?

Suddenly, in a startlingly spontaneous act of devotion, in the middle of the meal, Mary took a box of costly ointment, poured it over Jesus' feet, and wiped them with her own hair. Martha said nothing. Even the fact that Mary had unbound her hair in the manner of loose women and had used it to wipe Jesus' feet in the manner of slaves brought no rebuke. Perhaps while it was not in Martha's nature to do a thing like that, she, too, was consumed with thanks for the restoration of Lazarus and applauded Mary's action.

Some other references in the gospels to similar events are of concern here. Is Mark referring to this same occurrence in his gospel (14:3-9)? Why doesn't he name that woman then? He locates the event in Bethany, and the supper he describes could have been made by Martha in Simon the leper's house. But there is one profound difference in the two accounts. John says that the ointment was poured on Jesus' feet; Mark says it was poured on Jesus' head.

Pouring oil on the head has some startling implications. That's the way kings were set apart (see 1 Sam. 16:3,12; 2 Kings 9:3). Jesus was the "Christ," the Greek translation of the Hebrew word that means "messiah" or God's "anointed one." Did Mary now understand the full meaning of her sister's confession (John 11:27)? And if he were the "Christ," the "anointed one," why had no one ever anointed him?

John remembers that she had truly anointed Jesus, but did he forget that she had anointed his *head?* On the other hand, does the writer of Mark remember only the anointing of the head and consider the feet unimportant? If the stories are really about the same woman, Mary of Bethany, then both are important. The pouring of oil on the head will be remembered as the only messianic anointing Jesus received while he walked this earth, and the washing of his feet became a foretaste of his own footwashing of the disciples before his death (John 13:1-17). At that time he refused to let any of the others do for him what Mary had done.

Mark does not identify the persons who object to the act of generosity, but John says that Judas Iscariot was the one who, motivated by greed, bemoaned the fact that all of this money was wasted when it could have met some of the needs of the poor. Palestine certainly had its share of poor people, and nobody was more aware of their needs than Jesus, but in this instance he who "became poor" for our sake (2 Cor. 8:9) had need of the ointment.

Once again Jesus gives Mary his approval and rushes to her defense. "Let her alone," he tells Judas, "let her keep it for the day of my burial." Mark, considered the first gospel to be written, says it this way, "Let her alone; why do you trouble her? She has done a beautiful thing to me . . . she has anointed my body beforehand for burying" (Mark 14:6-8).

Then, writes Mark, Jesus makes this remarkable pronouncement: "And truly, I say to you, wherever the gospel is preached in the whole world, what she has done will be told in memory of her" (14:9). Nowhere else does Jesus make that kind of request of the future church. Should a memorial sermon be preached once a year to commemorate Mary's "anointing"? Should it be remembered in the same way his baptism is celebrated? What did Jesus have in mind as her perpetual memorial?

The Summary: Women as Contemplatives and Mystics

How we wish that Mary of Bethany had kept a journal and that her experiences had been preserved for us in literary form! Although her social experiences were limited by the restrictions of her day on the travels and works of women, her journey through her interior world, if recorded, would have enriched all of our lives.

People of Mary's temperament seem to understand intuitively the need for balance in the rhythms of work and rest. The Sabbath is a part of life and reflects the built-in human need for something more than work. As Thomas Merton, a modern-day comtemplative, once wrote: "I am not defending a phony 'hermit-mystique,' but some of us have to be alone to be ourselves" (*Contemplation in a World of Action*, p. 218).

We sense that Mary of Bethany was just such a person. Work for her was not an end in itself but that which needed to be done in order that a person might get on with the real business of living. For her, living meant reflecting on "every word that comes from the mouth of God" in order that she might give birth to new forms of witness and praise.

Within our being must be a place reserved for God alone, a place that, if given over to any person or thing, yields itself to idolatry. That God-shaped emptiness is fed by times of solitude and reflection. Out of such a center of devotion come such acts as Mary's ointment pouring, acts that are prophetic in their simplicity of meaning.

How else can we account for the fact that her action fulfilled an unmet need in the life of Jesus, a need she alone sensed as unmet? In solitude the intersection of the rational and the intuitive is made.

The history of the Christian church reflects the twin streams of scholasticism and mysticism. Through mystical experiences the human spirit partially fulfills its longing to be reunited with its Maker. Augustine said that we are made for God and that the heart is restless until it rests in God. This restless longing drives the mystic to seek a direct, intuitive encounter with God. The more rational, intellectual, scholastic, and dogmatic the theological climate becomes, the more the mystical experience will seek expression in the church.

Mary was a person of few words. Like other mystics she may have found words inadequate to describe the things she saw and heard. When writing to the Corinthians about his experiences in Christ, Paul struggled with the same inadequacies of language. "I know a man in Christ who fourteen years ago was caught up to the third heaven—whether in the body or out of the body I do not know, God knows. And I know that this man was caught up into Paradise—whether in the body or out of the body I do not know, God knows—and he heard things that cannot be told, which man may not utter" (2 Cor. 12:2-4). Paul could not even speak about his experiences in the first person but had to describe them as though they were happening to someone else. Language is so meager in its ability to describe our deepest feelings and understandings.

When we began Mary's story, we complained of the difficulty of writing about someone who said so little. Mary, like Paul, may have had difficulty expressing that which is ineffable.

Then, again, Mary probably did not know how to write. What a pity! We are denied any insight into her understandings of Jesus and his ministry with them. Mary will remain a profound mystery, a silent, reflective contemporary of our Lord. No wonder historians, even close to her time, have often confused her with Mary Magdalene and with the unnamed "sinner" of Luke 7 and with the unnamed woman of Mark 14! Medieval painters frequently identified Martha and Mary Magdalene as sisters (as we will learn in the next chapter), confusing Mary of Bethany with Mary of Magdala.

To the men who were given the privilege of communicating the gospel in the New Testament writings, Mary's actions were memorable while it seems that the woman herself was highly forgettable. It remained the task of later centuries, after women had learned to read and write, to give them a voice and a vehicle for communicating their profound insights into the nature of God.

Teresa of Avila has left us such insights. Fourteenth-century Catherine of Siena dictated her visionary experiences through a secretary. Jane Lead, a Protestant of the 17th century, used the language of mysticism to reintroduce us to dreams as the medium for spiritual understanding. Evelyn Underhill's books have become spiritual classics.

Not having Mary of Bethany's words or thoughts is our loss, but they still would speak less loudly than her deeds. Through her actions she has won for women of all time the right to participate in the learning and practice of theology.

Questions for Reflection

1. Now that you have met both sisters, with which one do you feel most comfortable? In the course of your reading about them did your feelings undergo any change? How?

2. Of what person in your circle of acquaintances does Mary remind you? What emotions are aroused in you by this association?

3. What do you think Jesus was saying to Mary while she sat at his feet? What questions would you ask him if you had the opportunity to learn from him?

4. Try to picture what life must have been like for the little family in Bethany after the raising of Lazarus. Have you ever experienced an event of comparable proportions in your family? How did it affect your conversations? Your plans?

5. Sometimes the words of Jesus in John 12:8 have been used to justify unconcern for the poor. How do you understand these words?

14

John 20:1-18; Luke 8:1-3
(Supplementary texts: Matthew 28:1-10; Mark 16:1-13; Luke
24:1-12)

MARY MAGDALENE

The Setting: Among the Women Who Followed Jesus

We step into the inner circle of Jesus' closest friends with Mary of Magdala. She was the leader of a group of women who journeyed with him on his preaching and teaching tours. In some healing way their lives had been touched by him. Whenever that group of women followers is mentioned, Mary Magdalene is always the first named.

Luke mentions some of these women by name and Mark mentions others. Among the women named in the group that followed Jesus are "Mary the mother of James the younger and of Joses, and Salome" (Mark 15:40); and Joanna, the wife of Chuza, Herod's steward, and Susanna (Luke 8:2-3). Both gospel writers also state that, in addition to those women, many others provided for the group of disciples out of their own means as they ministered to Jesus and followed him.

Luke apparently considered Mary Magdalene and the other women to be "disciples." In Luke 24:6-7, he quotes the angels when they remind the women that Jesus "told you, while he was still in Galilee, that the Son of man must be delivered into the hands of sinful men, and be crucified, and on the third day rise." Looking back to Luke 9:18-22, we note that this statement was made when "the disciples were with him" and he was praying alone. Apparently Mary Magdalene and the other women were there and heard the promise even as the angels reminded them. They were evidently counted among the "disciples" even though they were not of the Twelve.

The general designation "disciple" was also in common use after the resurrection and the Pentecost experience. At Joppa "a disciple named Tabitha, which means Dorcas," lived. So important was this disciple that, when she died, the rest of the disciples in Joppa sent for Peter, asking him "to come without delay." He came and called on her to "rise." She was restored to life so that she could continue to carry on her discipleship (Acts 9:36-42).

While the gospel writers differ in some details of their accounts of that first resurrection morning, they all agree on the presence of Mary Magdalene. Matthew tells us that she and "the other Mary" were at the tomb and saw one angel. Later on the way they saw Jesus. Mark has Mary Magdalene present with Mary the mother of James and Salome. In his first account one angel only appears to them, but Jesus does not appear. In an alternate account in 16:9-11, Mark says that Mary Magdalene *did* see Jesus.

Luke relates that Mary Magdalene was at the tomb with Mary the mother of James and with "Joanna," mentioned twice by Luke (8:3 and 24:10) but never in the other gospels. Two angels appeared to them, says Luke. John says Mary Magdalene was at the tomb alone, saw the stone rolled away, and ran to get Peter and John. While they were all together at the tomb, they saw nothing but the place where the body of Jesus had been, vacant except for the clothes that had been wrapped around his body.

Only when Mary Magdalene was alone, writes John (20:1-18), did the two angels and the risen Christ appear to her.

In each of the gospel accounts of the first Easter morning, one fact remains certain—Mary Magdalene was present and the first resurrection appearances were made to her. To her was given also the first apostolic commission to announce the good news of Christ's triumph over the grave (John 20:17-18). No wonder the theologian Augustine said that the Holy Spirit made Mary Magdalene the apostle to the apostles!

Given all the testimony of all four gospel writers, it becomes especially difficult to understand Paul's omission of Mary Magdalene in 1 Cor. 15:4-8, where he lists all those who saw the risen Christ. He seems to ignore all of the traditions concerning the presence of women at the tomb.

In her excellent study *The Women around Jesus* (Crossroad, 1982), author Elisabeth Moltmann-Wendel says that Mary Magdalene's preferential position and the conflict between men and women is more obvious in those gospels that were composed later and were not taken into the New Testament. In those writings, Peter appears a jealous rival of Mary Magdalene. In the *Gospel According to Mary Magdalene*, Moltmann-Wendel quotes Peter as saying, "Would the Redeemer, then, have spoken secretly with a woman without letting us know? Should we perhaps repent and all listen to her?"

Perhaps the Twelve never really did understand that Jesus was serious about the equality of all persons in his kingdom. Did they think that his speaking with the woman at the well (John 4), his gracious healings of women (Luke 8:40-56), his words denying that female anatomy was their "destiny" (Luke 11:27-28), and his appearances to the women at the tomb were accidents, mere coincidences?

Whether out of jealousy that a woman was the first apostle or out of a refusal to take the behavior of Jesus toward women seriously, the fact remains that the biblical writers make no further mention of Mary Magdalene after the resurrection.

The Story: The New Woman

(This section is based on the Bible account, scholarly sources, and personal reflection. Let your imagination help you to re-create Mary Magdalene's experience.)

What is the first word that comes to your mind when you think of Mary Magdalene? She evokes some strong associations in the minds of Bible readers, among them are words like resurrection, healing, demon possession, illness, wealth, dedication, friend, leader, but no one who reads the Bible carefully would ever associate the word "prostitute" with her. The association with harlotry many have made with Mary of Magdala cannot be found in Scripture.

History and the church have wronged Mary Magdalene. The sin of the Eighth Commandment claimed her as a victim and she is a prime example of its devastating effects.

Mary's call to follow Jesus came when he healed her, freeing her from demon possession. Demons were subject to Jesus from the very beginning of his ministry (Mark 1:23-27). Attacks of epilepsy, insanity, convulsions, blindness, deafness, and dumbness were all attributed to demon possession in Jesus' day. Now we know that many of these symptoms have other causes. (See Matt. 9:32-33; 12:22; 17:15-18; Mark 7:25-30; 9:17-29; Luke 4:33-35; 8:27-35.)

We are not told what the symptoms were in Mary's case. They could have been any of the above, but certainly there is nothing in the account of her healing (Luke 8:2) to indicate sexual uncleanness. Like the other people liberated from varieties of bondage by Jesus, Mary was changed forever. She became his devoted disciple, leader among his followers, constant companion of his journeys and his sufferings, and his personally commissioned messenger of the resurrection.

Before we deal further with the false reputation that has stigmatized Mary as a harlot, let's examine the nature of her call to discipleship. The holistic character of her commitment to Jesus is noted in Luke 8:1-3. While the male disciples were called away from various occupations, they had not experienced healings at the hands of Jesus. All of the women named as followers had been healed by him. In addition, they also left their families and followed Jesus just as the male disciples did.

The completeness of commitment was sealed by the women followers in their contributions to support the ministry of their Lord (Luke 8:3). Salvation demands total surrender from both men and women. When spiritual awakening happens in conjunction with physical healing, one's total existence is affected.

The Scriptures give us no clue as to Mary's age or marital status at the time of her call to discipleship. We do know that she had enough wealth to help support Jesus, and we know that she was a leader among the women. She seemed to have the strength of personality needed by women who, for perhaps the first time in their lives, were without the protection of their husbands or other male family members. (Note, for instance, Joanna, the wife of Herod's steward Chuza, who left her home to follow Jesus after her healing.)

But what about the prostitute tradition that has clouded Mary's history? We are confronting a mystery in this myth and are left to wonder why, alone of all the demon-possessed persons healed by Jesus, only Mary's demonism is attributed to sexual excesses? Why has she been identified with the woman in Luke 7:37, the "sinner" who kissed Jesus, anointed his feet, and wiped them with the hairs of her head? There is no biblical connection between the woman in the seventh chapter and Mary in Luke 8:2.

In fact, one finds on further investigation of the Scriptures that the poor "sinner" in Chapter 7 may have been just as falsely identified with harlotry as Mary herself has been. The Greek word for "sinner" and "sinful" occurs more than 40 times in the New Testament, but only in this one instance, the reference to the woman who was a "sinner" in Luke 7:37, has it been interpreted to mean sexual sin. One is left to question why, when women are associated with sin or demonism, their sin is considered sexual in nature!

Mary came from the town of Magdala, a city at the south end of the plain of Gennesaret. While Magdala was a wealthy city involved in trading, shipbuilding, and agriculture, it also had a reputation for licentiousness. Guilt by association may be to blame for Mary of Magdala's reputation.

In addition, some mysterious juxtaposition of the Luke 7 incident in the home of Simon the Pharisee and the Mary of Bethany story of John 12:1-8 has caused some interpreters to say Mary of Magdala and Mary of Bethany were one and the same woman. This theory has little to support it though. The passive, contemplative Mary of Bethany and the assertive leader of the women around Jesus are totally different in personality as well as in their histories. No mention of illness or healing occurs in any of the contacts between Jesus and Mary of Bethany.

One must regret the necessity of spending so much time clearing Mary Magdalene's name of its unsavory reputation rather than presenting her great strengths. (Certainly the regret does not arise from any need to clear Jesus of guilt from associating with women accused of sexual sin, since he obviously cared deeply about them. Remember the story of the woman accused of adultery and his loving treatment of her? [John 8:3-11]).

Mary of Magdala deserves to take her place in the history of our Lord's ministry as his close friend, the one who stayed with him throughout his sufferings and his burial (Mark 15:40,47) when all the other followers fled. John, the disciple who labels *himself* the one "whom Jesus loved" (John 13:23) nevertheless identifies *her* as the beloved friend for whom the first resurrection appearance of Jesus was reserved. The witness of her life was rewarded by the risen Lord with the first apostolic commission to preach the good news to the other disciples.

Let us remember Mary of Magdala as a friend of Jesus, faithful witness to his saving power, leader among the disciples, and the first preacher of the resurrection.

The Summary: Women as Preachers

In his book *Women Pastors*, O. John Eldred, a minister in the Ohio Baptist Convention, states that any search committee of a local church seeking a pastor can have confidence in the capability of women ministers to preach. School testing programs invariably demonstrate that females excel in verbal skills. The only thing they have lacked is the opportunity to develop those skills in public preaching and speaking. When given that opportunity they have demonstrated great ability.

Eldred cites some examples. Among politicians, Barbara Jordan, former congresswoman, impressed a nation with her keynote address at the Democratic Convention of 1976. Students of rhetoric are given the speeches of former congresswoman Shirley Chisholm to read as examples of excellence in speech. Catherine Booth, cofounder of the Salvation Army, preached to congregations of thousands before the era of public address systems. (Incidentally, she was also the mother of eight children!)

The resistance of Peter and the other disciples to the preaching and witness of women manifests itself in the same way today. The women reported the resurrection testimony of the angels, but the other disciples dismissed their witness as "an idle tale, and they did not believe them" (Luke 24:11). Jesus even rebuked some of them for not believing the report of the women with the words, "O foolish men, and slow of heart to believe . . ." (Luke 24:25; see also Mark 16:14).

Great courage is always required of those who testify to the bodily resurrection of Jesus (see Acts 4:1-3), and perhaps women face more ridicule and opposition than men. Attempts have been made to dismiss the fact that women demonstrated great courage by openly identifying themselves with Jesus at the cross and at the tomb while the male disciples were in hiding. Such attempts have been made with comments that the authorities didn't really consider women important enough to bother with them.

If that fact was true at the time of the crucifixion, it soon changed. We note from the account of Saul's (Paul's) persecution of Christians in Acts 9:1-2, that "any belonging to the Way, men or women" were subject to arrest and murder at his hands.

While Mary Magdalene disappears from the biblical record after the resurrection, her rediscovery as a preacher can be traced in 11th and 12th-century legends and stained-glass art in France. The tradition persisted that Mary Magdalene was the missionary saint to France. Moltmann-Wendel states that, according to the earliest legends, she was exiled from Palestine and came to Provence with her spiritual director Maximinus. Gradually his role diminished and hers increased.

Although the French have confused Mary Magdalene with Mary of Bethany, stained-glass windows in cathedrals in Auxerre, Florence, Lubeck, and Donaueschingen show her preaching, says Moltmann-Wendel. For a brief period in the Middle Ages before the Reformation, Mary Magdalene was remembered by the church in her preaching role.

Recognition of the preaching ability of women has revived in this century. In North America the Methodists, Baptists, United Church of Canada, Presbyterians, Disciples of Christ, and Episcopal and Pentecostal churches ordain women. Approximately 75 percent of Lutherans around the world ordain women to the preaching and pastoral office.

In February of 1970, some months before the Lutheran Church in America and the American Lutheran Church voted in their general conventions to permit the ordination of women, the findings of a scholarly research team were presented to the annual meeting of the Lutheran Council USA. In brief they said:

> In the past the Church has hesitated to ordain women because Scripture seemed to forbid it. Yet strict and literal enforcement of passages such as 1 Corinthians 11:2-16 and 14:33-36 has never been applied. In practice churches have given several kinds of leadership functions to women. Hence, and in the light of further examination of the biblical material, the case both against and for ordination is found to be inconclusive. (*The Ordination of Women*, Raymond Tiemeyer, p. 8).

Whenever we, as persons of this moment in Christian history, witness to the transforming power of the resurrection in our lives, we are following in the footsteps of our foremother and sister in the faith, Mary Magdalene. She who had encountered the living Lord in the restoration of body and spirit must have proclaimed the good news with great power. Our day, no less than Mary Magdalene's, demands the same kind of powerful personal testimony.

Jesus affirmed both the ability and the right of women to witness and to preach. Our call to do so comes from him.

Questions for Reflection

1. Mary Magdalene's healing is mentioned in Luke 8:2 and in Mark 16:9. Why do you think this event held such a prominent place in her biography?

2. What do you make of the fact that Peter and John went home when they saw that the tomb was empty while Mary stayed on in the garden?

3. Mary Magdalene added her personal testimony to the message Jesus sent to the other disciples (John 20:18). When might a Christian be justified in adding personal notes to the Word of God, and when might this be a violation of the message?

4. Never did Mary Magdalene deny or abandon Jesus. In fact, she may be called the first person to tell the news of the risen Christ. Why then do you think that she has been remembered chiefly as the penitent sinner, while Peter, who cursed and denied Jesus, is remembered as a great preacher (Mark 14:66-72; John 21:15-19)?

5. The close relationship between Jesus and Mary Magdalene is revealed in the delightful exchange of greetings between them (John 20:16). What insights does this give into the possibility of close friendships between Christian men and women?

15

Acts 18:1-3,18,24-26
(Supplementary texts: Romans 16:3-5; 1 Corinthians 16:19;
2 Timothy 4:19)

PRISCILLA

The Setting: Partnership in the Gospel

By the time we meet Priscilla, about 20 years had come and gone since the risen Christ appeared to Mary Magdalene. The fire and wind of Pentecost had appeared to the gathered multitudes, giving words of testimony to the disciples and opening the ears of the nations to hear them. The "church"—those "called out" to be the body of Christ in this world—had been scattered by the Pentecostal winds to proclaim the good news of Christ's victory to the world in which it was born.

The Spirit of promised power filled women and men alike, breaking down economic barriers and the barriers of race and sex (see Acts 2:17-18). Something so new had come into the world that Paul (then called Saul) had made it his mission to stamp out the followers of "the Way," convinced that they would destroy the religion he had been trained to uphold. He sought to arrest and imprison any men or women (Acts 9:1-2) belonging to "the Way," since it called all into discipleship.

Then Paul discovered that *he* was wrong and that the Christ of the Way was alive! He became a follower and a chosen and commissioned apostle of Jesus.

Under his leadership the Christian community mobilized its resources for missionary outreach and the establishment of communities of faith. The task required a "partnership in the gospel" with many men and women in all of the key cities of Asia Minor, northern Africa, and southern Europe.

In the earliest of his New Testament letters, written to the churches of Galatia, Paul waged war against the very doctrines he once defended. "You can't put people back under the law, those old legal requirements for holiness, once people have been made free and righteous in Christ!" (Gal. 5:1, paraphrase). And that means, says Paul, that "as many of you as were baptized into Christ have put on Christ. There is neither male nor female; for you are all one in Christ Jesus" (Gal. 3:27-28).

A new day had come for men and women (2 Cor. 5:17)! The apostolic church knew it and put into practice the order of redemption. So Paul sends regards and greetings to some of the women who labored with him in the gospel. In Romans 16 he begins by commending Phoebe as a sister in Christ and then goes on to greet Prisca, Mary, possibly a woman apostle named Junias, Tryphaena and Tryphosa, Julia, and the sister of Nereus.

In the letter to the Philippian Christians, he greets Euodia and Syntyche, women who "have labored side by side with me in the gospel . . . whose names are in the book of life" (Phil. 4:2-3). In Colossians, he greets "Nympha and the church in her house" (Col. 4:15).

As these biblical references seem to indicate, Paul considered women his partners. (You will recall our discussion in the session on the Samaritan woman of Paul's difficulty with the traditional role of women and of their new freedom in Christ.)

Phoebe is an outstanding example of an early church leader. Russell Prohl writes in his excellent study, *Woman in the Church*, that Paul gives both the title of *diakonos* and *prostatis* to her in Romans 16:1. Questioning why Phoebe is called a "deaconess" or "servant" in the translations, he says *diakonos* is used by Paul 22 times. Eighteen times it is translated minister, three times it is translated deacon, and only once, here in Romans 16:1, is it translated servant. (Note, the RSV uses "deaconess.") There can be but one reason for not using the common translation of the word as minister in this verse as well as in the others, and that is the fact that Phoebe was a woman.

The Greek word *prostatis* does not appear elsewhere in the New Testament but always means ruler, leader, or protector in Greek literature. In 1 Thess. 5:12, the verb form is translated "those who . . . *are over you* in the Lord." That Phoebe was in some sort of supervisory position seems quite likely.

The first "European" convert to Christianity was Lydia, a woman of Philippi (Acts 16:11-15). She was the head of a household and a businesswoman of some means. Through her initiative in inviting Paul into her home, she helped to open another continent to the good news of the resurrection.

We find ourselves living now in that new order that Jesus shaped (2 Cor. 5:17). Our journey through the Bible has given us intimate encounters with some of our sisters in the faith. We have walked with them this year on roads scarred with many trials, ennobled by triumphs over personal and societal obstacles and glorified by devotion to the God in whose image they were created. But a distinctive trait of the New Testament woman is her partnership with men (see Gal. 3:28). Her gifts, her skills, and her insights are absolutely necessary to fulfill Christ's mission in this world.

Women like Phoebe, Lydia, and Priscilla contribute to our understanding of women as leaders in the Christian church.

The Story: The Theological Woman

(This section is based on the biblical references to Priscilla, on scholarly sources, and on personal reflection. Let your imagination help you to recreate Priscilla's story.)

Priscilla and her husband Aquila probably came to Corinth around the year A.D. 50, refugees from political oppression in Rome. Both names are of Latin origin, but her race is not mentioned. She may have been a Roman by birth, but her husband Aquila was a Jewish Christian. It is known that there were Christian Jews living in Rome during the reign of the Emperor Claudius (A.D. 41-54). Claudius published an edict forbidding Jews to assemble together because of some rioting they were said to have been involved in. Since the practice of their religion required assembling, the only alternative for a devout Jew was to leave the city of Rome.

Since Priscilla and Aquila were tentmakers by trade, it was natural that they should become acquainted with Paul. In fact, since they were already living in Corinth when Paul arrived there, we might assume that Paul came to them seeking employment.

Apparently Priscilla and Aquila had prospered, because their house was large enough to accommodate Paul (Acts 18:3) and possibly a "church in their house." Wherever they lived, it seemed to be their custom to organize a congregation in their own home. (See 1 Cor. 16:19 and Rom. 16:5).

Paul would naturally look for the local Christian assembly whenever he came to a new city. Priscilla and Aquila were not only his partners in business but coworkers in evangelism and teaching. So close was their relationship that, when Paul left Corinth for Ephesus, after his arrest and trial before the proconsul Gallio, Priscilla and Aquila went with him (Acts 18:18-19).

Once again the couple were refugees. After his trouble with the Jews, their association with Paul could not have done their business in Corinth any good and they, too, may have felt it wise to leave that city. One way or another the Lord seemed to keep these witnesses on the move with the gospel. Paul soon left Ephesus to visit other cities and churches but Priscilla and her husband stayed there, no doubt organizing the church in their house and assuming leadership of the work in that city.

Life in both Corinth and Ephesus was corrupt, dominated by temples built to Greek goddesses. In Corinth, worship focused on the goddess of love, Aphrodite (Venus). In Ephesus, it was Artemis (Diana). Both temples and cities flaunted sexual promiscuity and a corruption of marriage. (Read Rom. 1:24-32, a letter written by Paul from Corinth, for a description of the corruption he was experiencing there.) The marriage relationship of Priscilla and Aquila was probably an impressive example of Christian love to the Corinthians who came to worship in their house church!

Their lives and leadership style seem to have motivated Paul to trust them with the leadership of the church in Ephesus. This leadership was challenged by the arrival in Ephesus of Apollos, and it is in the exchange between them that Priscilla's theological skill and Christian understanding are revealed.

Apollos possessed considerable biblical knowledge himself. In 1 Cor. 3:22 and 4:6, Paul implies that Apollos is of equal influence with himself and Peter (Cephas), and in Acts 18:24-25 his excellent credentials are listed. But apparently he did not know what Christian baptism was.

While he was preaching in the synagogue, Priscilla and Aquila went to hear him. Although he knew the Scriptures well and preached with great eloquence, they perceived that he lacked true understanding of God's grace in Christ and in baptism.

Why do we emphasize Priscilla's role in the correction of Apollos? It appears that Aquila and Priscilla had a marriage in which each one contributed certain gifts to the relationship. Sometimes Aquila is mentioned first, as in Acts 18:2 and in 1 Cor. 16:19. However, contrary to the custom of that time, Priscilla, the wife, is mentioned first in four instances (Acts 18:18, Rom. 16:3, and 2 Tim. 4:19). The most significant occasion in which she is mentioned first occurs in Acts 18:26 at the time of the Apollos incident.

In fact, John Chrysostom (A.D. 377–407), who often preached negatively about women, speaks highly of Priscilla. The fact that Paul greets her first, before her husband, impressed Chrysostom with its significance. He referred to this when preaching on 2 Tim. 4:19, and, when writing a homily on Romans, he said,

> It is worth examining Paul's motive . . . for putting Priscilla before her husband . . . (Rom. 16:3). He did not do so without reason: the wife must have had, I think, greater piety than her husband. This is not a simple conjecture; its confirmation is evident in Acts. Apollos was an eloquent man, well versed in Scripture, but he knew only the baptism of John; this woman took him, instructed him in the way of God, and made of him an accomplished teacher" (quoted in Leonard Swidler, *Biblical Affirmations of Woman,* Westminster, 1979, p. 298).

As a theologian Priscilla seems to have taken precedence over her husband and he deferred to her. Her reputation as a preacher and a teacher spread throughout the Mediterranean world. One of the oldest catacombs in Rome, the Coemeterium Priscilla, was named for her.

In her book *Foremothers*, Nunnally-Cox adds the note that a fresco of women celebrating the Eucharist was found in the Catacomb of Priscilla in Rome. It's possible that Priscilla herself was one of the celebrants in this portrait.

We do not know whether Priscilla had children. Perhaps not. She and Aquila may have been one of those couples who took seriously the imminent second coming of Christ, living by Paul's injunction to the Corinthian church that it would be better for persons to remain single "in view of the present distress" (1 Cor. 7:26) so as not to get bogged down by "worldly affairs" (vv. 32-35). Many Christians may have denied themselves children in order to give "undivided devotion to the Lord" (v. 35). Since no other effective method of birth control was available, Paul seems to advocate sexual abstinence for some couples (v. 29).

One tradition says that Priscilla and Aquila died as martyrs having their heads cut off. That cannot be proved or disproved, but we do know that they lived a life that demanded great courage. Paul tells the Christians in Rome to be thankful for these fellow workers in Christ "who risked their necks for my life" (Rom. 16:4).

The Summary: Women as Partners

Out of the New Testament there emerges the suggestion of a new living and working style for women and men, that of partnership in the gospel (Phil. 4:3). Add to that idea the gracious concept of "friends" (John 15:15), and the shape that emerges begins to look like the relationship between Priscilla and Aquila.

This couple evidently functioned as a team. They made tents together, they taught together, they traveled together, they risked their necks together (Rom. 16:4), and they organized and led congregations together! Their relationship may have found its basic proposition in Eph. 5:21, "Be subject (submissive) to one another out of reverence for Christ." If couples are trying to find a model of an equal partnership marriage, Priscilla and Aquila provide them with one.

Although they probably had arguments and occasional tension like every couple, they knew who was their "head," their Lord Jesus Christ. They were both subject to him, both devoted to his kingdom and his gospel.

In many Protestant churches, the number of husband/wife clergy teams is on the increase. As more women enter the seminaries, a natural result will be marriages between pastors. These clergy couples will join the long line of missionary couples, teacher couples, medical couples, farmer couples, and the many other teams that have modeled dual career marriages of the Priscilla-Aquila variety.

Equal partner relationships need not be confined to married couples. Whenever men and women work together, partnerships are on the increase. John Naisbitt, author of *Megatrends*, said in an interview that we are starting to abandon hierarchies that worked effectively in the centralized, industrial era. Now, he says, businesses are moving toward the network model of organization and communication, a more egalitarian form because networks restructure the power and communication within an organization from a vertical to a horizontal flow.

Instead of singing "We are Climbing Jacob's Ladder," author Matthew Fox suggests in *A Spirituality Named Compassion* that we start dancing "Sarah's Circle." Value should be placed more and more on gifts and skills than on degrees and offices.

In our journey from the story of Eve to the vignette of Priscilla, we have come full circle. In the story of the Garden of Eden, Adam and Eve were a team. They had equal responsibilities and equal opportunity for good and evil. Sin broke their relationships with God and each other. One sign of that alienation may have been a dominating/submissive relationship (Gen. 3:16b).

God's intention, however, was to redeem humankind from brokenness and alienation and to restore men and women to partnership and friendship. Priscilla and Aquila model so well a couple who worked side by side. Like Adam and Eve, who worked together in the garden in fellowship with God, they earned their living by working together, as tentmakers, in partnership with each other and with God. All of life was shared. They were one in the Spirit and one in their activities.

We have seen the destructiveness of sin and brokenness; in Christ we can rejoice in the possibilities for the wholeness that the cross brings to all relationships.

Our sisters of the Word, gifted women of faith and spirit, have shown us the way.

Questions for Reflection

1. Priscilla, Aquila, and Paul earned their own living while organizing the church. Do you think this model for ministry has any application for today (Acts 18:1-4)?

2. Priscilla and her husband were refugees from persecution in Rome. What contacts have you had with recently resettled refugees? With sanctuary for persecuted peoples?

3. We don't really know people until we have lived with them on a daily basis. How might Paul's relationship with Priscilla and Aquila been strengthened through living in their home?

4. Hospitality was essential to first century missionary outreach. Think about the difference between "entertainment" and the kind of "hospitality" practiced by Priscilla and Aquila (Acts 18:3 and 26). Do we need more of that today?

5. What do we learn about constructive criticism from Priscilla and Aquila's encounter with Apollos? What do the results of their confrontation tell us about their methods (Acts 18:26-28)?

FOR FURTHER READING

The following books were very helpful to me in the writing of *Women of Faith and Spirit*. I appreciate the stimulation that came to my own spirit as I read the writings of these sisters in the faith.

Emswiler, Sharon Neufer. *The Ongoing Journey: Women and the Bible*. New York: Women's Division, Board of Global Ministries, The United Methodist Church, 1977.

Moltmann-Wendel, Elisabeth. *The Women Around Jesus*. New York: Crossroad, 1982.

Nunnally-Cox, Janice. *Foremothers*. New York: The Seabury Press, 1981.

Reuther, Rosemary and McLaughlin, Eleanor. *Women of Spirit*. New York: Simon and Schuster, 1979.

Schüssler Fiorenza, Elisabeth. *In Memory of Her*. New York: Crossroad, 1983.

Wahlberg, Rachel Conrad. *Jesus According to a Woman*. New York: Paulist Press, 1975.